Power Up

Aspirations Ro

Book Three

By Mike Surowiec

Print Edition: ISBN 9798223300267

Power Up With Jesus - Aspirations Rooted in Christ! Book Three
By Mike Surowiec
Copyright 2023 by Abbaco LLC

Table of Contents

Introduction 1

#241 - Why Make A Commitment? 3

#242 - More Prayer, Greater Opportunities, Better Choices 4

#243 – Problem-Solver..6

#244 - Marriage, Dancing, Day Trading..7

#245 – Doing Church...9

#246 – You Can Defeat Satan's Influence 11

#247 – Form or Substance... 12

#248 – Spirit and Truth 13

#249 – Repentance 15

#250 – Little Faith 17

#251 - What Are You For? 19

#252 – Yellow Pencils 21

#253 – Knowledge 23

#254 – To Know God 25

#255 - Belief & Character.. 27

#256 - Getting in the Way of God's Spirit 29

#257 - Earn, Give, Save, Invest, Spend 31

#258 – Three Times 33

#259 - The Resurrection.. 35

#260 – The Cross... 37

#261- Entitlement 38

#262 – Dancing with God.. 40

#263 – God Speaks... 42

#264 - Helmets, Seat Belts, Armor 43

#265 - Financially Interdependent.. 45

#266 - Selfishness or Self-Interest?... 47

#267 – Sin Stinks... 49

#268 – Rejection 51

#269 – Idols 53

#270 – Advice or News... 55

#271 – The Book That Understands You 56

272 – Faith of Christ 58

#273 – The Pride Trap 60

#274 - Salvation: Relationship or Commodity? 62

#275 – Relate or Influence 64

#276 – Being Fully Human 66

#277 – Separation 68

#278 – Theology 101 70

#279 - Beaten, Busted, Broken 72

#280 – Who Before What or What Before Who? 74

#281 - Living in God's Presence 76

#282 – Preach What? 78

#283 – Tweet Gospel 80

#284 – Sin or Adoption 82

#285 - Christian Crutches 84

#286 - Let Christ Lead 86

#287 - Learning to Govern 88

#288 - Savior, Messiah, King 90

#289 – Feelings 92

#290 - "You Are Invited" 93

#291 – Fiat Character 95

#292 - Poor in Spirit 97

#293 - Inherit The Earth 99

#294 - Why Read The Bible? 101

#295 - Turning The World Upside Down 103

#296 - God, Family, Character 105

#297 - Jesus, Merciful Judge 107

#298 – Is God Unsafe? 109

#299 – JOB-I-TIS 111

#300 – Let Your Work Worship God 113

#301 – Free at Last 115

#302 - Twenty Minutes, Twenty Days, Twenty Years 117

#303 - Rules, Principles, or Character 119

#304 - Let Love Lead in the Marketplace 121

#305 - Who Are You? 123

#306 - Jesus is King 125

#307 - Living Dangerously with Integrity 127

#308 – Christian..129

#309 - Lean On Him (LOH) 131

#310 - Truth. Reality. God. 132

#311 - Is Money The Answer? 134

#312 - Where is Church? 136

#313 – Work..138

#314 - Follow The Money...140

#315 - Growth Involves Discomfort 142

#316 - The Ultra-Lean Years 144

#317 - Undesirables of Jesus 146

#318 – Good Work...148

#319 – Who Jesus?..150

#320 - Measureless Goals 152

#321 - How Do We Draw Near To God? 154

#322 - Lead People; Manage Systems..156

#323 – Making All Things New (Christmas) 158

#324 - Business is a Ministry 160

#325 - Segmentation or Coherence? 162

#326 - Kingdom of God in the Marketplace 164

#327 - Jesus the Carpenter...166

#328 - God's Plan For You 168

#329 - Jesus Wows Me Again 170

#330 - Blessed Test or Repeat...171

#331 - The Principle of Three...174

#332 - Making Decisions 176

#333 - The Joy of Business 178

#334 - Oops: Too Far?...181

#335 - The Greatest Blessing...184

#336 - The Flourishing God 186

#337 – The Suffering God 188

#338 - The Enjoyable God 190

#339 - Enjoy Life 192

#340 - Joy of the Lord..194

#341 - Being Aware of Our Need for Jesus Christ..........................196

#342 - Blessed and Broken..199

#343 - Thievery Against Marriage 201

#344 - Who Do You Trust? 203

#345 - If You Are Spiritual, Whose Spirit Do You Follow? 205

#346 - Witchcraft in the Marketplace 207

#347 - How Do Idols Hurt You? 209

#348 - Religiosity 211

#349 - Because I Can 213

#350 - Happy Birthday! 215

#351 - Want to Become A More Effective Christ-Follower? 216

#352 - Sin: Problem or Symptom? 218

#353 - Four Godly Attributes of a Successful Business 220

#354 - Is Your Jesus Dead or Alive? 222

#355 - Bless My Business 224

#356 - How About Blessing Those You Are With? 226

#357 - How Do You Measure Success? 227

#358 - What Do You Mean Ask, Seek, Knock? 230

#359 – Lonely Hearts 232

#360 - With God or Without God? 234

Other Books by the Author

Unequally Married
Simply The Messenger
Stay Free...Avoid Worldly Traps
Great Business Emulates a Good God
Dancing With God: Life-Giving Theology Explained
Overflowing Prayers Rooted in Jesus Christ v1 & v2
The Adventurous Journey of Transformation in Christ

Dedication

To my fellow apprentices in Christ who are intentionally living out the vision of God's Kingdom.

Scriptural Integration

"We continually ask God to fill you with the knowledge of his will through all the wisdom and understanding that the Spirit gives," (Colossians 1:9)

Introduction

The below Scriptures emphasize our Source of power.

<u>Acts 1:8</u>

But you will receive <u>power</u> when the Holy Spirit has come upon you, and you will be my witnesses in Jerusalem and in all Judea and Samaria, and to the end of the earth."

<u>Romans 15:13</u>

May the God of hope fill you with all joy and peace in believing, so that by the <u>power</u> <u>of the Holy Spirit</u> you may abound in hope.

<u>1 Corinthians 2:5</u>

so that your faith might not rest in the wisdom of men but in the <u>power</u> <u>of God</u>.

<u>1 Corinthians 4:20</u>

For the kingdom of God does not consist in talk but in <u>power</u>.

<u>2 Corinthians 12:9</u>

But he said to me, "My grace is sufficient for you, for <u>my</u> <u>power</u> <u>is made perfect</u> <u>in weakness</u>." Therefore I will boast all the more gladly of my weaknesses, so that the <u>power</u> <u>of Christ</u> may rest upon me.

<u>Ephesians 3:16</u>

that according to the riches of his glory he may grant you to be strengthened with <u>power</u> <u>through his Spirit</u> in your inner being,

<u>2 Timothy 1:7</u>

for God gave us a spirit not of fear but of <u>power</u> and love and self-control.

These aspirations were originally published on my blog. They are now bundled together in one place for a more convenient read. Book three is a continuation of the series (#241 - #360). Each aspiration gives you a greater glimpse into the heart of Jesus Christ as the Holy Spirit works to mold us into HIS image. As these lessons have done for me, hopefully, they will also open your eyes and mind to capture God's vision for your life.

As you read, ask God to enlighten you further. To make His Kingdom and ways a daily practice. Also, as HE opens doors for you, learn from the experience.

Along the way, may your relationship with the Triune God grow deeper and more trustworthy. You will also find as you grow in the grace and knowledge of Jesus Christ, your soul will more and more reflect HIM unto eternity.

My prayer is for Lord Jesus to intercede for you. To have Father God empower HIS Spirit to fully engage with you so you may experience the power of HIS Ways in your daily walk with HIM.

As always, we are rooting for you in Christ!

#241 - Why Make A Commitment?

"Jesus said to him, 'No one who puts his hand to the plow and looks back is fit for the kingdom of God.'" Luke 9:62

Without commitment, rarely anything good happens for the long term. Without commitment, there is no personal growth.

Without commitment, trust is questioned.

Without commitment, goals are only dreams.

Without commitment, love doesn't bloom.

Without commitment, friendship is shallow.

Without commitment, the business is surely to fail.

Without commitment, a marriage is only a negotiable contract.

Without commitment, God is only an idea.

Without commitment, treaties between countries is a fantasy.

Without commitment, laws are only a suggestion.

Without commitment, excellence is never obtained.

Without commitment, accountability is waived.

Without commitment, faith is an illusion.

Our Triune God sets the standard for commitment. He made the commitment before the foundation of the world to birth a new humanity (Ephesians 1:4). No matter how often mankind messes up the process, He is always faithful. HE reveals His commitment each day. How about you? What is your commitment level?

#242 - More Prayer, Greater Opportunities, Better Choices

"And this is my prayer: that your love may abound more and more in knowledge and depth of insight," Philippians 1:9

Want to improve your love life? Your career? Your financial house? Pray!

Prayer is the means we commune with the Great Designer. The same Being who is Love, who enjoys work, and knows our basic necessities as a human being.

His desire is to share His life in you, with you, and through you. But he is respective of your boundaries. He will not force you to follow his desires. Rather he wants you to willfully choose to be in a meaningful relationship with Him.

Prayer is the means he designed for that purpose. It is heaven's cell phone. You have direct contact with your heavenly Dad who wants his children to succeed in life.

It doesn't take a college degree. Nor an introduction by a high ranking official. Or a specific position for him to hear you. It only takes a willing heart. A heart that wants to be in a relationship. A heart that wants to learn and grow in the relationship.

As you venture into the area of prayer, you will discover a new addiction. One that helps you view life through the same eyes of the Man-God that walked the earth 2,000 years ago. You will begin to see opportunities that weren't there before. You will make choices with a more long-term horizon. You will experience the joy of walking in the presence of your heavenly Dad.

It happens when you live a prayer-full life.

#243 – Problem-Solver

"When Jesus saw him lying there and learned that he had been in this condition for a long time, he asked him, 'Do you want to get well?'
'Sir,' the invalid replied, 'I have no one to help me into the pool when the water is stirred. While I am trying to get in, someone else goes down ahead of me.' Then Jesus said to him, 'Get up! Pick up your mat and walk.' At once the man was cured; he picked up his mat and walked." John 5:6-9

How can we best preach the gospel without using words?
Be a problem-solver!

Ever noticed how Jesus related with people who he first met? He first started out to determine the problem. Then shared his resources to resolve the problem. Afterward he would present God's word on the matter.

Review the gospel accounts yourself. See for yourself how Jesus solved the problems of others. Every solution increased his credibility and created a platform for him to preach.

So why not do the same in your business and relationships? If you want to be a little Christ, preach the gospel without words. Discover their problem and solve it! As you gain credibility, opportunities will present themselves. Then you may share the gospel message with a few words for an attentive ear.

#244 - Marriage, Dancing, Day Trading

"What gain has the worker from his toil? I have seen the business that God has given to the children of man to be busy with. He has made everything beautiful in its time. Also, he has put eternity into man's heart, yet so that he cannot find out what God has done from the beginning to the end. I perceived that there is nothing better for them than to be joyful and to do good as long as they live; also that everyone should eat and drink and take pleasure in all his toil—this is God's gift to man." Ecclesiastes 3:9-13

The best things I learn about life and walking with God comes from three activities. They are marriage, ballroom dancing, and day trading.

Marriage is the platform that introduces me to self-sacrificial love and mutual submission. The same love Jesus demonstrated is put in practice within the marriage relationship. The same attitude apostle Paul writes about is tested each day within the bounds of marriage. Marriage cultivates the fruit of godliness within a relationship. Why? Because Christ is the center of the two. If I can't make it work in marriage, how do we make it work elsewhere?

Ballroom dancing teaches me to lead others by mutually working together on the same goal. Whether we are dancing the foxtrot, waltz, or polka, it doesn't matter. We are sharing the rhythm and count in an organized, expressive manner. It is a joy to experience. Most often the male leads. But when professionals dance, the lead role may switch back and forth. The casual outsider may not even recognize when.

In my early dancing attempts as a young man, I had many a widow move me around the dance floor. They knew I wasn't ready to lead. I was happy to learn. Later in life, I learned that there is a time to lead and a time to let the other lead. Insecurity and control are the demons that prevents one from experiencing mutual satisfaction. The same problem may carry over when following the lead of the Spirit in one's life. Dancing teaches me the joy of mutual leadership.

Day trading the future markets involves risk and reward. But when one's trading strategy involves reality, repentance, and boundaries, one succeeds. To trade successfully, one needs to recognize what they may not initially see. That the market is greater than any one person and deserves a high amount of respect. Realizing its power, we need to change our thinking towards it. We need to relearn everything we think we may know about it. In a sense, we need to repent and believe in its possibilities. In the process, we need to develop boundaries to protect us from harm. Only then will one experience the fruit of success.

The trade masters from yesterday have much to say how to manage our relationship with this beast. For some this god is cruel and mean robbing them of their livelihood. For others, the god is a rewarder of those who praise and respect it. For those who learn to live within its boundaries, you will live to trade for another day.

I chose to learn from the masters of yesterday. Those who have successfully walked and thrived against this god. Likewise, I love to read the Bible. Why? To learn from those who have gone before me.

The market has taught me how to respect the Triune God. When I grasped His reality, repented and changed my thinking about Him, life improved. I learned to walk within His Divine boundaries. Life became immeasurable more than breathing, eating, and sleeping.

Now you know why I have a soft heart for marriage, ballroom dancing, and day trading. They remind me of my relationship with our Triune God. How about you? What activities make God come alive in your life?

#245 – Doing Church

"For where two or three are gathered in my name, there am I among them." Matthew 18:20

When I initially submitted my first dissertation proposal the Chair turned me down. The paper was on "Doing Church." In his opinion, the subject matter was too vast and the research too difficult. His recommendation was to find another topic more easily digested. I did. Yet the subject of doing church still intrigues me.

When most of us think of church, we picture a building or an institution. In America we may even think of a legal corporation. Some of us may associate church with a specific denomination. Others are more open.

When we think of how church is conducted, most of us will associate a church service as the only way of doing church. Yes there are a variety. The Catholic Church is heavy on liturgy and visual stimulation. The Greek Orthodox likewise have their rituals and traditions with a short message. The Protestants have their contemporary music with a more lengthier message. The Amish and Mennonite's have a more yesterday act. Yet, how many other ways are there to do church?

What has intrigued me is how Church functions more than a meeting held in an official place. When one understands the Church is a Body of people (Eph. 1:22-23) who come together to worship God, the venues become worldwide.

When your family comes together with a heart and mind focused on God, is not Church in session? When two or more of you come together in the workplace in the Spirit of serving God and man, isn't Church in session? When you are driving on the freeway with a fellow believer with a heart to glorify God, isn't Church in session?

The fact is Church encompasses more than most of us ever contemplated. How Church Service can be conducted is even more than what most of us will ever practice.

So the next time you are in the marketplace, ask yourself. How can you best glorify God through your work, relationships, and deeds? In so behaving, are you not doing Church?

#246 – You Can Defeat Satan's Influence

"...Resist the devil, and he will flee from you." James 4:7

What is Satan's Mission?

Jesus stated that Satan was a liar and murderer from the beginning of human history. That his mission is to steal, kill, and destroy. (John 8:44, 10:10)

Satan's chief tactic hasn't changed over time. He uses deception, doubt, and pride to turn your heart and eyes away from God.

He is an artist at twisting the truth. He makes promises built upon human pride. He questions God's intentions by bringing Him down to a human level. He loves to cause disunity. Rebellion and enslavement are his tools.

How do we eradicate him from our lives? We can't. He roams around seeking someone to devour. But what we can do is make his influence ineffective. We resist his advances. We walk in the authority of Jesus Christ who has already defeated Satan.

Like Jesus before us, we need to know scripture and the Truth it represents.

When confronted by Satan's craftiness, we need to resist by turning to God.

We don't flirt with Satan's lies. We don't negotiate with Satan's deceptions. We don't even argue with him. Instead we resist; protected by the armor of God.

The Bible teaches us that when we resist, Satan flees. Satan can't handle those who don't play along with him.

#247 – Form or Substance

"Beware of false prophets, who come to you in sheep's clothing but inwardly are ravenous wolves. You will recognize them by their fruits. Are grapes gathered from thorn bushes, or figs from thistles? So, every healthy tree bears good fruit, but the diseased tree bears bad fruit. A healthy tree cannot bear bad fruit, nor can a diseased tree bear good fruit. Every tree that does not bear good fruit is cut down and thrown into the fire. Thus you will recognize them by their fruits." Matthew 7:15-20

Ever wonder why a package is larger than the item inside?

We recently purchased an item from my favorite online store. When the box arrived, I questioned whether it was for me. I didn't recall ordering anything that large. Upon opening the box, I recognized the item. My new computer mouse. The item was less than 10% the size of the box!

Once with one of my former employers, I recall arguing who to hire as our new receptionist. The owner wanted the young, very attractive lady who modeled on the side. I wanted the excellent communicator who had a history of getting things done on time. I lost the battle, but eventually won the war. When he discovered she couldn't spell nor manage phone calls, we replaced her. We soon hired the person who had more substance than form.

Likewise, notice how politicians emphasize all show, but fall far short from deliverables. Again, more form than substance.

2 Peter chapter two highlights how Christians can identify false teachers. We will know them by their fruit. The emphasis is on character. In this case, form takes a second seat to substance.

So, don't get over excited by the package. First recognize what is inside. If the heart, mind, and soul shouts with Godly character, than accept the substance with the form. Otherwise, beware.

#248 – Spirit and Truth

"God is spirit, and those who worship him must worship in spirit and truth." John 4:24

How does one worship in spirit and truth? For spirit is a matter of the heart and mind. Truth pertains to honesty and transparency within reality. How does that translate into practical, everyday means?

Most Church services have a time for worship. A time typically surrounded with the sound of song and music. For many church-goers, this is worship.

Yet is this what Jesus meant when he informed the Samaritan woman that we are to worship in spirit and truth?

Worship is much more than a twenty minute session of song and music. In fact, for some it may not even be a time of worship. If one's heart and mind is not focused on God but on "enjoying the moment," is that worship? If one is preoccupied with what others are doing, is that worship? Does worship require song and music?

The fact is worship is our offering to God. It is aligning our spirit with his. It is being honest with oneself in relationship with the living God. It is positioning oneself in total awe and reverence at the feet of the God of Creation.

The means we worship God is as variable as the personalities, talents, and gifts found in the Body of Christ.

Yes we can worship God through song and music. But we can also worship God in silence and stillness. We can also worship God in our work, hobbies, and recreational pursuits. We can worship God in our service for others. We worship God whenever we show him our gratefulness and thankfulness.

When we are open, honest, and real with him we place ourselves in a vulnerable position showing our trust in him. Whenever we acknowledge him during the day we are worshiping him.

Whenever you place your heart into his hands you are worshiping Him. Whenever you speak the truth, you are worshiping him. Whenever you offer him praise and thanks, you are worshiping him. The time or place doesn't matter. What matters is the motive of your heart and mind plus your word and deed. When you direct your all for HIS glory, not yours or anyone else's, you are worshiping HIM.

So the next time you speak, think, work, and play, stop and ask yourself, how can I worship God with this activity?

#249 – Repentance

"Thus it is written, that the Christ should suffer and on the third day rise from the dead, and that repentance and forgiveness of sins should be proclaimed in his name to all nations, beginning from Jerusalem." Luke 24:46-47

So many religious words. What do they really mean? Take repentance. Most of us growing up in the Bible belt associate repentance solely with sin. Whereas Jesus stated repentance (*metanoia*) and forgiveness of sins are two distinct subjects.

Repentance has to do with changing your mind. In today's vernacular, it is to change your worldview.

It is to acknowledge Jesus Christ is Lord and King and Savior of heaven and earth. It includes renouncing sin, but so much more. It involves being reeducated. It is learning life from the Triune God's perspective. It involves questioning everything you have learned from the world's system. Then comparing it to how God sees it and does it.

Like Saul who was zealous for the traditions of his father's we also need to change our worldview. He went from murdering Christians to becoming one. He changed his entire viewpoint of life after encountering Jesus Christ. He even changed his name from Saul to Paul. We likewise experience the same through repentance.

Repentance involves our beliefs, values, and traditions. It is a complete house cleaning of one's soul and mind.

John the Baptist preached about the repentance of sin. He did so until he died. Jesus then fulfilled his initial destiny on earth. He died for us removing the eternal death sentence (past, present, and future sins) from us.

Repentance is acknowledging what He did. Admitting that we have been wrong about him. Than moving toward focusing our mind, heart, body, and soul for HIS glory. It is leaving behind what we were before we came into contact with Him. It is allowing His Spirit to change us from the inside-out. It is acknowledging we are poor of spirit. That we need His involvement to permanently change our hearts to match his.

Repentance is so much more than eliminating the practice of sin from one's life. It is aligning ourselves with the Triune God's divine order and perspective. It is the process of adding God's worldview into your world. This leads to a refocusing of your time, talents, and treasury. When God becomes the center of your life, you can't help but be thankful and grateful for everything He has done. Plus what HE is doing. It all begins when we repent.

#250 – Little Faith

"For truly, I say to you, if you have faith like a grain of mustard seed, you will say to this mountain, 'Move from here to there,' and it will move, and nothing will be impossible for you."
Matthew 17:20

How much faith do you need to live a productive life as a Christ-follower? Whenever I hear people state that we need more faith, I cringe. My reason and encouragement comes from Jesus himself. He rejoices over the fact that we have "little faith." His claim is with very little faith we can move mountains.

There is no shame to have only "little faith." Faith is faith. Look at Jesus' statements in regards to having a little faith.

"One who is faithful in a very little is also faithful in much..." Luke 16:10

His master said to him, *'Well done, good and faithful servant. You have been faithful over a little; I will set you over much. Enter into the joy of your master.'* (Matthew 25:23). Doesn't He provide for us who have 'little faith'.

We have learned over a lifetime that God is good and faithful. He always delivers on time and in the best method possible. Over the years we have also learned that it is not my faith but His faith that helps me through life's ordeals. Also as we pray and ask, we don't know specifics of how or when. All we know is God produces good. And whatever happens is God taking everyone into consideration. It may not always be best for me (my opinion). But it is best for the advancement of His Kingdom.

For example, whenever we have a mountain blocking our path, what do we do? Don't we wait patiently for God to provide a solution? Isn't it a challenge to wonder how God is going to do it this time? In prior times, he may have sent a person to help us through. He may have "dropped a meteor out of the sky" to miraculously have the mountain flatten. Or he may have simply given us a shovel to start digging. Through the process we build character and strength. He may even allow our great-great grandkids to continue the process. He may want them to enjoy the thrill of having the mountain finally disappear. He doesn't always reveal his plans to us. He deals with the issue in a way that we all know He handled the productive outcome. And we are grateful for his involvement in our life.

I for one am thankful that my little faith is more than enough that allows us to walk with our heavenly God. So if you have little faith - REJOICE.

#251 - What Are You For?

"For we are his workmanship, created in Christ Jesus for good works, which God prepared beforehand, that we should walk in them." Ephesians 2:10

Do people know you by what you are for or what you are against?

In no particular order, but as defined from a Biblical perspective, and as an apprentice of Jesus Christ, I am for...

The Triune God

Jesus Christ

Kingdom of God

Holy Spirit

Love

Joy

Peace

Patience

Goodness

Kindness

Gentleness

Faithfulness

Self-Control

Humility

Excellence

Knowledge

Understanding

Wisdom

Truth
Healthy Relationships
Respectful Boundaries
Marriage
Family
Justice
Unity
Worship
Service
Stewardship
Life-Giving events
Grace-filled situations

There are more, but these attributes are the building block that I hope others see. They reflect the character of God. Hopefully, this is a major part of the brand noticed by others wherever and whomever I meet. How about you? What are you for? What are you broadcasting to others?

#252 – Yellow Pencils

"For by the grace given to me I say to everyone among you not to think of himself more highly than he ought to think, but to think with sober judgment, each according to the measure of faith that God has assigned. For as in one body we have many members, and the members do not all have the same function, so we, though many, are one body in Christ, and individually members one of another. Having gifts that differ according to the grace given to us, let us use them..." Romans 12:3-6

What would life be like if everyone only wrote with a #2 yellow pencil? We probably would manage. Yet, what would happen if someone introduces you to a red pencil? a mechanical blue pencil? a typewriter? a computer? Which would you prefer?

One of the challenges of leadership is surrounding yourself with people complimenting you. There are leaders who surround themselves only with people who are like themselves. In my time we called them "yes" people. They always would agree with leadership in public. But behind doors, they totally disagree with the leaders final decision. They act like they are 100% behind the decision, but passively rebel when the foot hits the cement.

Then there are leaders who surround themselves with all types of people. Many who differ from themselves. Abraham Lincoln built his senior cabinet surrounding himself with people of high abilities. But whose allegiance would be questioned from the outside looking in. Yet he recognized that differences of opinion and personality are important. So he surrounded himself with people of many attributes. They would assist him with reaching important decisions.

What does this have to do with yellow pencils and the church? Sometimes we in the church believe everyone should behave and act and look in a peculiar way. Like yellow pencils, we think unity comes from conformity on the outside. We tend to forget Christian unity comes from the Spirit (Ephesians 4:3). Ever notice how ministers from the same seminary behave and act similarly. They simple execute what they have learned. Like yellow pencils, they look and act accordingly.

Yet there are those who realize the purpose of a pencil is to communicate through the written medium. The color of the pencil doesn't matter. Whether it is a #2 or a #3 pencil doesn't matter. What matters is that the message is communicated.

I am thankful God created us with different personality, ethnic origin, and attributes. It adds flavor and color into the action. Yet for those whose preference is yellow pencils; I am also thankful that God created you. Without you I wouldn't appreciate all the various differences that make up the Body of Christ.

#253 – Knowledge

"An intelligent heart acquires knowledge, and the ear of the wise seeks knowledge." Proverbs 18:15

Today we work in the age of the knowledge industry. History has already recorded the agricultural, industrial, and technological periods. They have come, are still with us, but are not the leading industry now. The industry that leads today is in the knowledge arena.

Those who know are paid for what they know, not what they actually do. Those who best acquire, interpret and apply the information are the leaders of industry.

Most of us in business understand the importance of gaining head knowledge. But the more successful entrepreneurs also realize the importance of heart knowledge. As an apprentice of Jesus Christ, we are likewise to grow in the knowledge of HIM (2 Peter 3:18).

As Jesus' apprentices, we are instructed to gain knowledge. Not superficial know-how, but knowledge to transform our worldview (Romans 12:2). Likewise, as we abide in Christ, our hearts are being renovated after our Chief Mentor (2 Corinthians 3:18). This comes via the Spirit as we walk through the challenges of life.

Most of us either have a bias to pursue one or the other. We either invest time to gain head knowledge or emphasize heart knowledge. The fact is we need both. As the book of 2 Peter outlines, we are to grow in the grace & knowledge of Jesus Christ. Grace is a byproduct of experiencing the work of the Spirit in our life. Knowledge is coming to know Jesus Christ in a relational perspective. As we do, we will grow both in head and heart knowledge.

So no matter your natural preference, realize we need both. As we pursue both, we place ourselves in the position to grow in the grace and knowledge of Jesus Christ.

#254 – To Know God

"But if anyone loves God, he is known by God." 1 Corinthians 8:3

What is life all about? The question has been debated over eons of time by every philosopher and want-a-be. As I gracefully age and look back at life, the answer becomes more focused: To Know God. To know is more than head knowledge. It is the head and heart and willpower mutually focused on the Source. The God I speak about is the same one Jesus revealed to all.

He is not a God who roams somewhere in heaven and doesn't intervene into history unless invited. That is the God of some. But my God is involved in every aspect of life. Whenever and wherever and whatever we do, God is there. When you wake up in the morning, God is there with you in the shower and at the breakfast table. When you drive to work, God is with you. When you perform you work, God is there. When you stop at the gym on the way home, God is with you.

When you work out a math problem, you come to know more about who God is. When you discover more about science, you come to know more who God is. When you do your debits and credits and reconcile your check book, you discover more of who God is. When you listen to a song on the radio, you learn more about who God is. Everything we do reveals more of who God is. Yes even when we see or experience evil or sin, we discover more of who God is and is not.

When Jesus Christ becomes the center of your life, your worldview begins to change. You begin to view the world from God's perspective. You begin to recognize HIS work. You begin to come to know him better even as he knows you. Together, you learn to dance through life's obstacles and challenges.

It all begins when you learn to love him with all your heart, mind, and strength. When you do you begin to see him in every aspect of life. You see him after disasters. You see him in the middle of a crisis. You see him celebrate life's good moments. You come to know him and grow with him.

Yes the older I become, the more everything in creation reveals His character, heart, and mind. We spend our lifetime discovering more of who HE is in everything we do. So the next time you find yourself in the middle of a project, ask yourself. "What are you discovering about God that you didn't know before?" Your world will never be the same.

#255 - Belief & Character

"For this very reason, make every effort to supplement your faith with virtue and virtue with knowledge, and knowledge with self-control, and self-control with steadfastness, and steadfastness with godliness, and godliness with brotherly affection, and brotherly affection with love. For if these qualities are yours and are increasing, they keep you from being ineffective or unfruitful in the knowledge of our Lord Jesus Christ." 2 Peter 1:5-8

Over the years I marvel at how God works within people's lives, including yours truly. Most of the time, He comes through not on our schedule, but His. The process rarely repeats itself. Though if there is something uniquely being creating within us, then it may. Then there are people who believe God will instantly move mountains from their life. But reality seems otherwise.

Fiat. Immediately. No sweat. Convenient quick results is not standard operating procedures for a Jesus apprentice. Now God does produce miracles. He also does answer prayers immediately. But, there are situations when He extends the outcome for our sake or for the sake of others. There is not one method or formula that fits all when it comes to God.

What I find in my life and in many others is God has more in mind than immediate resolution of a problem. Most of the time, He opens the door that will create growth opportunities for you, me, and those around us. In most cases, those challenges are not what we want, but what we need.

Like 2 Peter states, HE is building character within our soul. HE wants our faith supplemented with attributes of HIS character. Real character. Character built on the foundation of Jesus Christ and not self, vain glory. A life secured by an eternal foundation rather than a humanistic platform.

So how does little faith move mountains? Yes, God can move it without any help. But like many of his solutions, we may need to grow in character. He will lead us through the solution, but it may take time. He may bring an earthquake, an explosion, or a super strong wind. But most likely he will bring people into your world that will help you. The final solution is not as important as our obedience to walk in our small faith trusting Him.

So hang in there. With God, mountains do move.

#256 - Getting in the Way of God's Spirit

"You stiff-necked people, uncircumcised in heart and ears, you always resist the Holy Spirit. As your fathers did, so do you." Acts 7:51

Stubbornness, which is a byproduct of pride and a heart that amplifies the self, has been the ruin of many people. Stephen, a martyr for Christ, spoke this Scripture at the religious leaders of his day.

The problem which he identifies is the same one today. Many of the religious and non-religious people today ae groped by stubbornness. I group them together because the issue is the same. They both have a hard heart and are convinced that their way is the only way of living a prudent life.

The religious person likes to emphasize the rules, the principles, and the methods. Whatever makes them feel good about themselves must be good for others. If it works for them, it must be good for everyone else.

The non-religious person sees through their game playing. But likewise imitates them by throwing out the baby with the bath water. They see the hypocrisy and don't want anything to do with it. Instead of focusing on Jesus' message, they look at the misdirected behavior. They close their eyes to everything else.

Both sides miss the mark of realizing the problem is within them. As one person stated somewhere, " when we point a finger at someone, three fingers point back at oneself".

Jesus once stated during a teaching moment, that a person pure in heart will see God (Matthew 5:8). Most of us don't look for God's involvement in a situation until after the fact. By then, a difficult situation has become a worldwide crisis. Always ask, seek, and knock from the beginning. Why wait until your effort and resources are wasted. Begin to seek help from God at the start.

A Christ-Follower looks past the human condition. She walks in the presence of the Triune God. She generally is able to distinguish God's work from man's facade of righteousness. The reason is because that is where they came from. It takes one to know one.

The Holy Spirit is always at work. It is the Spirit that gives life (John 6:63). Like the wind, we may not see him, but we see the impact. Yet, we need to be attuned to HIM. We need to realize God has given us a new heart (Ezekiel 36:26) that allows us to communicate and share in his fellowship. As we walk with Father-Son-Spirit, our harden hearts are displaced with a new heart. God's gift opens the pages of HIS universe and allows us entrance into HIS presence.

So the next time you think you are doing right, stop and ask God for confirmation. You may be surprised with an answer that is more favorable for all involved parties. And yes, it is possible that you may not be initially correct.

So be a person with an open, attentive heart plugged into the Holy Spirit network. Be aware of HIS revelation. God has a way to change one's opinion and worldview quicker than any other method. Or do you want to be known as the person who resists the work of the Holy Spirit?

#257 - Earn, Give, Save, Invest, Spend

"I am the LORD your God, who teaches you to profit, who leads you in the way you should go."
Isaiah 48:17

If you are starting out in your career, now is the time to put in place a financial formula that works. Those of us with finance degrees or experience have a basic foundation. Yet, what is lacking for most are life-giving values. In most cases, we learn the hard way - through our poor decisions. A better way is from the success and mistakes of others.

Warren Buffet, one of the wealthiest men in the world, began his career by living on 50% of his earnings. He did so for over twenty years while investing the difference. John D. Rockefeller, one of the wealthiest men in his time, used a similar approach to life. My mom and dad, hard-working immigrants with only an eighth grade education, exercised a similar formula. They were able to send two children to a private school. Plus, pay off their house in five years, and enjoy retirement debt free.

Their formula was the same as many other financially successful people. They lived on less than they made while investing the difference. A simple strategy. But few in today's culture are able to discipline themselves to practice. Yet those who practice it, appreciate the results.

The ideal is too find something you either enjoy doing or are good at to earn a livelihood. As the income comes in, the lust is to start spending on everything you desire. Don't. Instead start by allocating money from your first paycheck. Focus on the long-term important goals and not desirous wants of your life.

Start by asking God where HE wants you to share his income with. Whatever he instructs you, follow through. It most likely will be your local church. Yet HE may also suggest a para-church ministry or a nonprofit. That is doing good work in serving humanity from God's perspective.

Wherever it is, God enjoys a cheerful giver (2 Corinthians 9:7). Start off by giving a percentage that you can do so cheerfully. Some in the church preach the discipline of giving a tithe or ten percent as a starting point. If you can do so cheerfully, do it. If you can give more, do it. If you can only give less, do it. Whatever the amount, I assure you God overtime will transform your heart. You will become more generous in your giving. It is all HIS anyway. We are only learning to behave as HIS stewards.

Next, start saving. Whatever % amount you give away for a cause greater than yourself, save the same % amount. Keep doing so until you reach 6 months of your annual income. It may take a few years, but when you arrive, you will have reached a point of economic freedom. If anything happens to your job, you have a reserve to fall back on. If an emergency arises, you have assets to fall back on. You won't have to live paycheck-to-paycheck any longer. You will then have an emergency reserve.

After reaching your six month savings plan, start investing. Study and become a student of investment. If you are not adept at investment, than hire a personal planner without an agenda. Let him/her direct you into the instrument that will take your money and let it grow. There is no better way to earn a living than making money from money. That is how the rich live.

But you say by following the above, I will have to deny myself immediate pleasure and desires. Yes. But the fruit will taste better in the long run. Ask Warren Buffet. Ask my parents. Ask those people now in the late season of life. Many spent their money without saving. If they could do life over again, ask them what they would do differently.

The Bible states the borrower is a slave to the lender (Proverbs 22:7). That there is profit in all labor (Proverbs 14:23). God knows how money is best invested (Ecclesiastes 2:24-6). These principles are true today as they were 3,000 years ago when first written. Yes, it takes faith to deny the self now for the potential of a better future. So are you ready to make the faith journey with your economic life? It all starts when you earn, give, save, invest, and then spend.

#258 – Three Times

"Three different times I begged the Lord to take it away. Each time he said," My grace is all you need. My power works best in weakness." 2 Corinthians 12:8-9

How do you know when you have prayed and received confirmation from God?

There are scriptures that state we should continue to pray and ask and never quit (Matthew 7:7). This is true. Persistence and patience is rewarded by our Lord. Yet when you receive the same reply three different times, you may consider it time to accept the answer.

For example, we don't know the specifics of Paul's request (2 Corinthians 12:8) except that it was a pain to his flesh. Some think it may have something to do with his eyes. Others feel it may have been a demon assigned to agitate him. It could also have been some other chronic ailment. Who knows how many traumatic beatings his body endured. He was a survivor of many shipwrecks and confrontations. What it specifically was doesn't matter for our purpose.

He asked and received the same reply three times. Rather than continue to make requests unto the Lord, he accepted God's answer. He in obedience and faithfulness moved forward.

Another example is Jesus Christ himself. On the night he was betrayed (Matthew 26), he spent three hours making three requests with His Father. He wanted to find another way to fulfill the mission. Yet after the third prayer, He accepted His Father's answer and the rest is history.

After his resurrection, Jesus met with Peter (John 21) and asked him three times whether "He loved Him." Though this was for Peter's sake, who recently denied Jesus, now Peter confirms that he loves him.

Peter also witnessed the same vision three times (Acts 10). The outcome confirmed the Lord's decree that all men are included in His work of salvation.

Three identical replies seems to be the number for confirmation. So if you are looking for confirmation from the Lord, you now know when to stop praying and start obeying.

#259 - The Resurrection

"Blessed be the God and Father of our Lord Jesus Christ! According to his great mercy, he has caused us to be born again to a living hope through the resurrection of Jesus Christ from the dead,..." 1 Peter 1:3

What are the three "R's" that came from Christ's resurrection?

The first "R" is Reconciliation (Col. 1:19-20). Humanity divorced God when Adam & Eve rebelled against Him. But He initiated the first steps and completed the process of reconciliation. The divide between mankind and Himself was restored through the work of Jesus Christ.

The second "R" is Renewal (Titus 3:5). After Jesus' resurrection, He fulfilled his promise of providing us with a Comforter. HE will not only direct us into all truth, but will renew our hearts into the image of our Creator.

The third "R" is Restoration (I Peter 5:10). God continues to show HIS purpose to restore life to his original intent. Throughout Israel's history and Jesus' ministry HIS actions displayed the same. Ever notice when Israel collapsed into darkness, God pulled them back. When people came to Jesus for healing, he would restore their health and life back again. God has been and is in the restoration business.

This Easter, you may want to take time out and read chapter fifteen of Corinthians. Paul writes in greater detail what the resurrection means to us. He summarizes the meaning of Jesus' resurrection. He describes its impact into our personal lives. My suggestion is prayerfully read it. Ask God to open your mind and heart to capture the vision and meaning in your life today.

And yes, there is an unofficial fourth "R". It is a Reminder that God created us to enjoy life in Him, with Him, and for Him. Happy Easter!

#260 – The Cross

"For the word of the cross is folly to those who are perishing, but to us who are being saved it is the power of God." I Corinthians 1:18

What happened on the Cross the day Jesus died?

The sacrificial system stopped.

The broken relationship between God and humanity was restored.

The guilt and shame of the fall was replaced with freedom and liberty.

The war of good over evil was won.

The human race was redeemed from Satan.

Grace now triumphs sin.

God strategically outwitted Satan.

This is a simple reminder for those of us that sometimes forget. Or take for granted the impact of Jesus' life & sacrifice.

#261- Entitlement

"...all things were created through him and for him." Colossians 1:15-17

Where are we taught that the world owes us something? That government, church, or business exists to please our desires? What does life owe us besides our existence? Are we entitled to fulfill all our dreams? These are some questions people may ask from the position of "what's in it for me?"

Like a spoiled child, some believe all their desires and dreams are to be instantly gratified. When they are not, they become emotionally belligerent. They turn their resentment against whomever has denied them their "rights." Whether it is our boss, mate, parent, government, and yes even God. Yet, like a repented spoiled child, many learn over time to appreciate and be grateful for what they have. But for most of us, it takes time for the heart to morph into a channel of thankfulness.

One day all will know this world was not made for you nor I. The Bible states the world was created for Jesus Christ. We are his invited stewards.

It is Jesus Christ who surrendered his eternal home on a mission for his Father. He exercised faith and courage. He fought the battles of life to overcome Satan, sin, and death. He substituted His vicarious life for ours. He redeemed humanity from their initial rebellion against grace. His victory is humanity's win. He earned the right for supreme leadership as King of all kings and Lord of all lords. He is earth's and heaven's ultimate Ruler and Judge.

So what are we entitled too?

How about the opportunity to live? Yes, even though the quality and quantity of life is limited by many outside factors. For example, being born in a favorable family or government increases one's odds for a better life. Yet, there are no guarantees under the sun. The results of what we pursue and chase after may or may not occur. Only physical death is absolute. (Some say taxes, but if you have no qualified income, taxes are avoidable). Thus, the only thing we are entitled too is the opportunity to live and die.

Everything else is only because of God's unmerited favor. God's grace makes life more enjoyable. Those who have chosen to accept his authority also have the guarantee of the 1st resurrection. Otherwise, all other perceived entitlements are desires that blind and rob us. They steal us from a more intimate relationship with our Creator. HIS blessings are more than enough to handle in this life.

#262 – Dancing with God

"You have turned for me my mourning into dancing; you have loosed my sackcloth and clothed me with gladness," Psalm 30:11

Before "Dancing with the Stars" show, ballroom dancing was only for the old timers. When I went out, my date and I were always the youngest on the dance floor. But we learned and had fun. To move our bodies within the framework and rhythm of the big band sound of the 1930s, was a good entertaining time. But it didn't happen overnight.

In high school, I was the quiet, silent type who hid behind a wide smile. Though backward and inept in many ways, I made up my mind to change. It started at the weddings.

I found out early in life if you treated the ladies with respect and charm, you could always find a dance partner. It took a while. But I became comfortable to move into their territory without fear or intimidation. While sitting at the family table with the band playing, I would look for the girls who didn't have dates. Then I would join them at their table. Start a conversation. That led to explaining my desire to learn how to dance. Most often the girl would offer to teach me. Though I stepped on many a foot and tripped over my steps more often than not, they taught me as their #1 mission in life. That is how we started.

In my early twenties, I was also fortunate to date a couple of young ladies who likewise loved to dance. Whenever their dance partners were unable to go out that weekend, they would call me. They knew I wasn't the best, but was an able learner. We spent many a night at the Polish, German, and Italian culture clubs. Plus the big band indoor and outdoor nightclubs. We learn to polka, swing, cha-cha, and fox trot. In the beginning they would lead and I would follow. Soon thereafter, I developed to the point where I led and my partner followed.

So what does this have to do with dancing with God? Everything. I find our relationship with the Triune God is one large dance. That Father-Son-Spirit move together like two partners on a dance floor. They move individually yet mutually together. That same togetherness is how God wants us to follow Him.

God leads, we follow. Individually, yet mutually together. In sync with the divine music. Sometimes it's a fox trot. Other times, it is a swing. Then it's a slow, hip-hop, tango. Whatever the beat, He leads, we follow. Together, the movement is one intimate, fulfilling dance that brings out the best in you and I.

So when someone now asks me what a relationship with God is like, I tell them. It's a Great Dance. He leads, I follow. In the process, I experience the thrill of moving around the world's dance floor. HE holds me in HIS grip. We sway to the divine music He orchestrates throughout the day. Yes, life is one Great Dance with the Almighty. Would you like to join us?

#263 – God Speaks

"Whoever is of God hears the words of God. The reason why you do not hear them is that you are not of God." John 8:47

How many different ways does God speak to us?
The Bible is the means most evangelical Christians claim God speaks to us. This is true. Yet, is it the only way?

How about in prayer? (Psalms 66:19)

How about in our dreams? (Matthew 2:12)

How about through visions? (Luke 1:22)

How about through angels? ((John 20:12-13)

How about through other people? (Jeremiah 35:15)

How about through a burning bush? (Exodus 3:2)

How about through secular poetry? (Acts 17:22-31)

How about through creation? (Romans 1:20)

There are probably other ways that don't quickly come to mind. So if you can add more to the list, I would love to hear from you.

Bottom-line: don't limit the way God speaks with you. He only wants an attentive, believing heart that is available to listen.

#264 - Helmets, Seat Belts, Armor

"Finally, be strong in the Lord and in the strength of his might. Put on the whole armor of God, that you may be able to stand against the schemes of the devil. For we do not wrestle against flesh and blood, but against the rulers, against the authorities, against the cosmic powers over this present darkness, against the spiritual forces of evil in the heavenly places. Therefore take up the whole armor of God, that you may be able to withstand in the evil day, and having done all, to stand firm. Stand therefore, having fastened on the belt of truth, and having put on the breastplate of righteousness, and, as shoes for your feet, having put on the readiness given by the gospel of peace. In all circumstances take up the shield of faith, with which you can extinguish all the flaming darts of the evil one; and take the helmet of salvation, and the sword of the Spirit, which is the word of God, praying at all times in the Spirit, with all prayer and supplication. To that end keep alert with all perseverance, making supplication for all the saints," Ephesians 6:10-18

A strong defense wins championships.

This statement has been repeated by sport teams over the years. Yet how does that apply to everyday life?

This past week, I had a bicycle accident. The bike tires hit what this northern transfer calls "rubber ice." For those outside the state of Florida, rubber ice is the result of rubber mats placed on sidewalks. Their purpose is to prevent people from slipping on the pavement. Yet, a problem occurs after a rain shower when the rubber mat becomes wet. When bicycling, one must approach these mats directly head-on. Otherwise, you risk having the tires spin out of control.

The latter is what happened when I quickly turned onto the sidewalk at an angle. The tires didn't hold and the bike went into a slide. When everything stopped, I was a pretzel caught under the bike. My cheek rubbing the cement ground. Thankfully, I was wearing a helmet which took most of the blow to the head. I was fortunate to walk away with only minor scrapes and bruises.

I recall another incident in those early years driving the car. While on the service drive of a freeway another car ran a stop sign and broadsided me. The impact knocked my car off the road toward the freeway which laid approximately 30 feet below. The impact knocked me from the driver side to an upside down position on the passenger side. When the car came to a stop, my head was on the passenger floor mat and my feet upright hitting the ceiling. My right hand though hung onto the steering wheel. This kept the car from toppling off the service ramp some 20 feet below into oncoming traffic.

Again, I was fortunate to walk away with bruises and minor cuts. This was before the law of the land required seat-belt usage. Anyway, after that ordeal wearing a seat belt became my standard MO. This happened before it was even the law.

Today, wisdom recognizes the importance of wearing helmets when cycling. Plus seat belts when driving cars. One never knows when outside circumstances could cause an accident with crippling results.

The apostle Paul writes in Ephesians the defensive measures for a Christ-follower. The safety measures are to prevent catastrophe against the devil's ploy. He described them as the whole armor of God. It includes Truth, Righteousness, The Gospel, Faith, Salvation, Word of God, and Prayer.

If you want a strong defense, then learn, understand, and integrate each of these tools into your life. The world's circumstances will test you through unexpected battles. To survive and endure to the end requires putting on defensive gear. Always best to have on before an unplanned accident occurs. With the proper equipment, one has a better chance of walking away with only minor bruises and small cuts.

Those who walk without protective gear risk the impact of an accident's fury. Whether bicycling, driving, or navigating life's jungle, it is better to practice safety. The armor of God helps you to manage the risk of the unexpected.

#265 - Financially Interdependent

"As each has received a gift, use it to serve one another, as good stewards of God's varied grace" 1 Peter 4:10

One of the most challenging decisions to make is accepting God's offer of joining Him in his work. Until then, we operate under the illusion of self-sufficiency. This is especially true for those who are wired to create wealth in the marketplace.

This is generally why a person is not satisfied with his first million or billion. Or the person seeking intimacy through more sexual conquests. Or the parent that feeds their self-image through the accomplishments of their children. These people manipulate for his or her personal desires rather than what is best for others.

Many of us are generally motivated because of some traumatic event early in life. We are driven to pursue a course thinking that the outcome will please our inner hunger. But after we arrive, we find our self still hungry or hurting. Then in our blindness we continue for more. We act this way because we still hunger and hurt. We follow the path of more when in reality we need less.

But when a person comes to the realization God owns it all. That HE only lends us resources for our good and for the good of others. Only then will we appreciate the vastness of His domain and influence in our life. The Bible reiterates that God owns it all. That we are HIS children working in the family business. We are under His domain. We acknowledge his authority in our life. We gladly provide the hands and feet in partnership with HIM to serve, to grow, and to flourish with others. All this under the domain that HE has given us.

That domain may include only one person. Or that domain may be a family; or an organization, community, or national chair. The size of our responsibility does not matter. What matters is our realization. That we are in a joint venture with the King of Kings to restore this planet to His original intent. Under such a scenario, accountability takes on a greater meaning than satisfying oneself.

When money comes before God, Houston has a problem (as NASA would state). When God is there only to serve our money dilemmas, we have a problem. But, when we accept our Kingdom role as a bond-servant, we are glad to offer our services to further His purpose. We are thankful for any opportunities HE gives us. In fact, we look forward to express the talents and abilities He has bestowed upon us for His glory.

At the end of day, we acknowledge that all the wealth, treasures, and bank accounts are his. We are only his stewards. We provide the hands and feet; he provides the resources. Together we share a life experience. We of course get the best side of the deal as He bestows His grace upon us for his namesake.

#266 - Selfishness or Self-Interest?

"You shall love your neighbor as yourself." Mark 12:31

Somewhere we may have forgotten the difference between selfishness and self-interest.

Jesus stated that we are to love our neighbors as our selves. Yet we are told not to be self-centered. How can one be interested in the self without being self-centered?

Simply defined: self-interest recognizes the self is a person. Made in the image of God. And is important in God's domain.

Selfishness though, is when we only recognize our own personal desires and needs. Selfishness does not take into account the interest of others.

Without the protection of self-interest, we become pawns manipulated by others. Even Jesus said that we are to be harmless as doves but as wise as serpents when dealing with the world.

A person generally behaves with their personal agenda the center of life. Unless the Holy Spirit is actively involved. With the Spirit of God one begins to view life from the others perspective. That includes God's view and the people around us.

The Spirit reminds us that all have been justified through the life and death of Jesus. That we can be a witness for others. We can work with the Spirit for the sake of others as they learn to accept Jesus as their Boss. Until then and thereafter, we are to be concern with our brothers and sisters. We are to take care of them as we want others to take care of us.

As children of God's Kingdom, we are to follow the lead of the Spirit in our life. We are to include God and others in our decisions. And when push comes to shove, we deny ourselves for God's glory and for the sake of others. It is not all about me. It is about God, others, and me.

#267 – Sin Stinks

"You come to the help of those who gladly do right, who remember your ways. But when we continued to sin against them, you were angry. How then can we be saved? All of us have become like one who is unclean, and all our righteous acts are like filthy rags; we all shrivel up like a leaf, and like the wind our sins sweep us away. No one calls on your name or strives to lay hold of you; for you have hidden your face from us and have given us over to our sins." Isaiah 64:5-7 NIV

Being a student of God's grace, I marvel at the Holy Spirit. How HE transforms us through the everyday occurrences of life tips my equilibrium.

Though God works with His children in different ways, HE also works with us in a similar fashion. Take Sin. A concept that is becoming outdated in today's modern world of humanistic faith. Yet sin prevails and is more real today than ever before.

Ever watch a newly converted child of God first learn about the Truth? What happens when his internal spiritual light bulb starts flashing? It is a refreshing joy to witness their first love. They can't find enough time to study the Bible. They want to inform everyone they meet what is happening in their life. They can't seem to express the love and joy that emulates within them. For us longtime disciples, it brings back memories of our first encounter with God.

Yet after the "first love phase" begins to dissipate, a new season of life appears. I call this the "sin stink's phase." It is when the Holy Spirit begins to convict a person of attitudes or behavior that is unbecoming of a child of God. All a sudden, a person begins to recognize in depth what is wrong in the world. They begin to associate the sin with the evil. They begin to see the problem around them and more so within them. They begin to acknowledge that they are part of the problem. That their pride, selfishness, and independent thinking fuels the problems of the world.

Then the Holy Spirit begins to illuminate the gospel message into everyday routine. Grace becomes real. Love becomes meaningful. Truth becomes personified. The life, death, and resurrection of Jesus Christ takes on a greater role than just a personal savior. His victory over Satan, death, and sin begins to have a greater influence in their life.

The focus now is not on sin and its ramifications. Instead one emphasizes the importance of living within the Triune God circle. Instead of beating a dead horse (sin), one begins to ride in the victory parade of the King (grace). Instead of participating in the problem, one begins to share the good news. For Jesus Christ is the permanent solution.

Yes sin stinks. But Christ dismantled sin's dominance. We now take part with Him in his victory march.

The Triune God wants humanity to recognize that sin stinks. That life at its highest level is living within the divine order of Father, Son, and Spirit God. Otherwise, why do you think God allows sin to hang around as long as it has?

#268 – Rejection

"As you come to him, a living stone rejected by men but in the sight of God chosen and precious, you yourselves like living stones are being built up as a spiritual house, to be a holy priesthood, to offer spiritual sacrifices acceptable to God through Jesus Christ." 1 Peter 2:4

You are included. These words are most encouraging when one begins to understand God's redemption plan.

For years, I thought God only loved me if I performed in a religious manner. If I went to church every Sunday. If I lit my candles. If I gave money. If I reduced the swear words from my mouth. God would be so satisfied. HE may even bless me with more than a so-so life.

When the good news of Jesus Christ first etched into my mind, I couldn't believe it. It sounded radical. Impossible. What is the catch? What strings are attached and conditions not being conveyed?

Growing up in today's culture, one is constantly being rejected. Could be your ideas. Could be potential relationships running into roadblocks. Business ventures turning south. From all such abuse, one usually becomes gun shy and defensive. We may build walls around our heart. Each rejection causes another defensive wall to cover up the pain. Eventually, we live with so many defensive guards in place. So many that we can't even experience life any longer. We live a shadow of who we were created to be.

We experience rejection through a multitude of events. Divorce and job terminations destroy relationships. Unwanted pregnancies, first love breakups, and sibling rivalry shatter our tender egos. The problem isn't rejection. It is our response.

If we are fragile without mature roots in Jesus Christ, we become defensive or offensive. Either approach though causes pain within ourselves or in others through destructive means. If we withdraw within ourselves, we cover up the hurt. If we live in denial, we are lying about the situation. If we attack the other party, we will only cause greater harm.

But, with mature roots in Jesus Christ, we follow the lead of our Rabbi. We forgive. We pray for the other person asking God to intervene and bless the other party. We transform rejection into the opportunity for good to come about. We lay it down at Jesus' feet and ask Him to intervene and make things right.

Generally speaking, rejection occurs when one of our idols fail us. The pain may hurt for a while. But instead of allowing rejection to damage us, we use the pain to allow God have his way with us and them. Not an easy thing to do without God. Humanly speaking, almost impossible for most. But with God, rejection becomes the cornerstone of a new beginning.

The process allows Jesus Christ's work of reconciliation to be continued. Our idols are dismantled. We grow as a person. Others are blessed through our prayers. God's domain expands. We learn to live in a healthy relationship with God, others, and self. Over time, we discover that rejection becomes the catalyst for something good. Only because Jesus made it and makes it possible.

#269 – Idols

"You shall have no other gods before me." Exodus 20:3

What makes something an idol? Why is an idol so destructive in your life? Or is God on an ego trip?

For the moment, set aside any religious understanding you may have on idols. And let's look at it from a practical point of view.

What was the first idol that appeared on the world scene? Would you believe it involved an archangel. The Bible states that God created Lucifer more beautiful than any other angel. But, rather than show gratitude to God and walk humbly with Him, Lucifer began to look at himself. He began to look at himself as superior to God. His pride turned himself into an idol. The result was a failed coup of heaven and banishment from authority within God's domain.

What was Adam's and Eve's sin? Didn't they make the forbidden fruit an idol? Rather than spend more time developing a relationship with God or Adam, her focus was on the fruit. Upon the Serpent's temptation, she allowed the idol to supplant her key relationships. She behaved like Satan before her. She wasn't satisfied in keeping the relationship between her and The Lord in place. She was created to be like God, but limited in her physical attributes. She wanted more. She wanted to be more like God and took circumstances into her own hands to make it happen. She wasn't going to wait for God to bring it about in his way and schedule. Her idol became her Achilles heel.

An idol is simply anything that comes before God. Generally speaking, idols really don't exist anywhere but in our hearts and mind. Whatever takes the place of God in our worship, love, and passion is a candidate to become an idol.

Some of the candidates that we convert into idols include money, power, and sex. Others are food, friends, family, country, politics, religion, and science. By themselves, they are usually neutral and generally very good for our well-being. But, whenever they become more important than God, we have crossed over into idol worship.

The result of idol worship is generally a kick in the pants. Idols are false strongholds that empower us away from God and reality. God has designed a divine order in how life works. When we build our life outside of HIS order, holes and craters will appear. The result is usually pain and sorrow and even premature death.

God created us. He made us to worship him. He designed us to walk with Jesus Christ. He encased us to have fellowship with the Holy Spirit. Like a marriage relationship, a mistress takes away the intimacy between the two. The same is true when an idol comes between our Heavenly God and ourselves.

You may not recognize the idols in your life. God does. He knows your spiritual condition. That is why I am most grateful for Jesus Christ. His act of justification and grace only demonstrates his awesome love for us. I for one am thankful that he cares enough for us that HE takes the time to help destroy the idols in our life. We may not like the process, but the fruit at the end of the day is most scrumptious.

#270 – Advice or News

"How beautiful upon the mountains are the feet of him who brings good news, who publishes peace, who brings good news of happiness, who publishes salvation, who says to Zion, 'Your God reigns.'" Isaiah 57:7

Dr. Timothy Keller states it best. Especially when you compare the difference between religion and Christianity. He likes to state that religion gives advice, but Christianity is good news.

Religion is about working to improve the human condition via self-help. Whereas Christianity is accepting the fact Jesus Christ has already completed the act. One is based on performance. The other is simply accepting the fact it is done.

The news that God's grace is enough; that our obedience is only showing our gratitude to Him, is Good News. When we start with giving advice, we are sliding into the religious camp. When we obey because it makes us feel good about ourselves, we are crossing over into the religious zone. When we perform acts in exchange for blessings, we are playing religion.

The Good News is that Jesus Christ is our savior. HIS life, death, resurrection, and ascension completes the work of salvation. We now take part with him in his work of redemption, reconciliation, and restoration. He leads; we follow. We belong to him and submit to his authority. He is the Good News that we faithfully accept. Apart from Him, there is no good news. But more advice.

#271 – The Book That Understands You

"The unfolding of your words gives light; it imparts understanding to the simple." Psalm 119:130

Ever read a book you couldn't put down? Especially when the author wrote it knowing everything there is about you. She knew what excited you. She took you from an emotional high to a painful low. She knew what got your goat. She knew how you thought. She knew what you would do next. She deliberately turned the next chapter against your perceived ideas. Everything about you that you haven't shared with another soul was in the story. Everything you ever thought, believed, or held true was being drawn out of you through each chapter of each page.

Now some people may shy away from such a novel. Others would want to read the sequel and couldn't wait until the story became a movie. Such a book would probably be a number one seller for years.

Some people may not be aware of it, but the Christian Bible has been a number one best seller each year it has been in print. It is a book that truly understands you and me. The book depicts violence, sex, and power. There is political intrigue, suspense, and surprise outcomes. In some cases, miracles and other unbelievable results. It showcases romance and rags-to-riches stories. You also read the difference one person makes in the lives of others. It captures human nature at its finest and worst. It explains how you are wired and what can be done to transform it. It is a story with more plots than a graveyard.

You want to know why you behave the way you do? Read the Book. You want to better understand why others are the way they are? Read the Book. You want wisdom in dealing with the people in your world? Read the Book.

You want your life to have greater adventure and excitement like the movies you enjoy? Read the Book. You want to develop a relationship with someone who totally understands you? Read the Book.

As you read the Book you discover more about its invisible Author. You come to know the people who He associates with; the people who are drawn to him. As you read the Book, you begin to better understand yourself, your motives, and your potential. You learn better ways to relate with others. You become more like the heroes written in the Book. You understand their pain and joy because you share in the same venues.

The more you read, the more you realize Someone understands you better than anyone else. Then you begin to realize Who. Its prime Author created you. HE wants to have an ongoing, long term, intimate relationship with you. It begins when you read the Book!

272 – Faith of Christ

"Knowing that a man is not justified by the works of the law, but by the <u>faith of Jesus Christ</u>, even we have believed in Jesus Christ, that we might be justified by the <u>faith of Christ</u>, and not by the works of the law: for by the works of the law shall no flesh be justified." Galatians 2:16 KJV

So many translations; so many different opinions. What is a person supposed to believe?

There is debate among Biblical scholars in regards to the verse in Galatians 2:16. They claim many Bible translators incorrectly translated the sentence. The correct verbiage is found in the King James Version. Newer Bible versions have altered the meaning by using the word "in" versus "of." (I have underline the two places above). The problem is the meaning. When we use the word "of" we are placing the emphasis on Jesus' faith. When the word "in" is used, we are placing the emphasis on our faith.

I will leave the scholarly details for those who are better trained to educate. Instead, I will go on record toward the KJV interpretation. Why? Because it makes more sense from a holistic basis.

If I am justified based on my faith, than what is the difference between human works of law and human works of faith? Both place an emphasis on saving oneself by oneself.

But, if I am justified by the faith of Christ, than it is not my work, but Christ's work. He made it all happen and grants us the grace to accept it.

My part is to believe in Him. He lived, died, and was resurrected on our behalf. He is the cornerstone. The faith or trust that I have in Jesus is because He did it, is doing it, and will do it. He made it all possible.

Even the faith that I have in him is a gift from him. Through the Holy Spirit, HE has empowered us to believe. Yes, I had to acknowledge that Jesus is who he claims to be. Yes, I had to ask for the Holy Spirit. And yes, I submit to the authority of the Father/Son/Spirit.

It is a relief that my tiny belief is being upheld by the faithfulness of Jesus Christ. Is not that a breath-taking, grace-filled, and life-giving fact? Doesn't that make one more thankful and grateful for our Triune God to share His life with us? And HE does so without heaping religious burdens on us. I for one am more at peace for placing trust in Jesus' faith than in my own. How about you?

#273 – The Pride Trap

"The haughty looks of man shall be brought low, and the lofty pride of men shall be humbled, and the LORD alone will be exalted in that day." Isaiah 2:11

Pride has been the downfall of many through human history. It is listed as one of the major sins of humanity (Proverbs 8:13). Overtaken by pride, Lucifer turned into Satan. His pride made him attempt a coup of heaven. Pride kept little ole' me from experiencing God's best throughout most of my early life. It is a heavy cost to carry.

If you don't think you have a pride problem, take another look. It doesn't matter whether you are rich or poor. Doesn't matter if you are formally educated or not. Does not matter if you are endowed with beautiful looks or not. Doesn't even matter if you are blessed with good health or not. Even if you are naturally gifted with a superb talent, it doesn't matter. Pride comes to all in one form or another. Generally, pride appears when we place ourselves or beliefs in a superior position. When that happens fire alarm sirens should blast loud and clear.

Pride builds walls that prevent effective communications. It is unable to love. It stumps emotional and intellectual growth. It hurts those around you and robs you of your joy. It has caused the ruin of relationships, businesses, and countries.

Pride glories in the self. It sometimes hides behind humility. It is often praised in the media. Ignored by those who should identify it and debase it. Its friends are few and destructive. Rarely nothing good comes from pride. The only exception is when its annihilated. Or when real humility is allowed to enter.

Pride is like the top of a housing bubble. The ride up may be temporarily enjoyed, but the fall is very troublesome by all who take part in it.

Pride can be broken. But it is best when replaced by a spirit of humility that comes from a Holy Being.

Yes, God loves us; even in our pride. In fact he loves us so much that He shares His Spirit to eradicate the pride of life from our most inner parts. We are to abide in Christ. As we do, we will become clothed with the humility of Jesus. Yes pride will occasionally lift its ugly head. But God has forgiven us way before that ugly pride ever showcased itself in our presence. That is why we are grateful for Jesus' work of redemption, renewal, and restoration. The longer we abide in him, the less pride manifests itself. It is replaced by His humility.

#274 - Salvation: Relationship or Commodity?

"...so that he(Jesus) might present the church to himself in splendor, without spot or wrinkle or any such thing, that she might be holy and without blemish. In the same way husbands should love their wives as their own bodies. He who loves his wife loves himself. For no one ever hated his own flesh, but nourishes and cherishes it, just as Christ does the church, because we are members of his body. "Therefore a man shall leave his father and mother and hold fast to his wife, and the two shall become one flesh." This mystery is profound, and I am saying that it refers to Christ and the church." Ephesians 5:27-32

Growing up in the 21st century within a capitalist culture is challenging. Especially for one to fully grasp the teachings of the Bible. Take for example the concept of salvation. Is salvation a commodity to be exchanged or a relationship to be experienced?

There are those who believe upon repentance one receives salvation. We exchange our repentance for a one-way ticket to heaven. Then there are those who believe salvation occurred approximately 2,000 years ago. When Jesus' death, resurrection, and ascension redeemed humanity. That upon accepting the reality of who Jesus is, we begin to experience the fruit of salvation.

I lean towards the second view. When we view salvation as a byproduct of our effort, we are treating salvation as a commodity. But, when we view salvation as an engagement, than we are treating salvation as a relationship.

The apostle Paul used the analogy of being engaged to Jesus Christ. In Paul's time it was the man who selected his wife-to-be. He would work out the arrangement with the woman's father. If the father approved, he gave his daughter to him. In a sense, the woman would wake up and discover who her husband is to be. She didn't choose her husband. It wasn't a decision she made. She simply acknowledged the reality that she was engaged to be married. Thereafter, she focuses herself in accepting the relationship of her husband-to-be. She accordingly changed her thinking and behavior to that reality.

Salvation is likewise an engagement in a marriage relationship. But we need to view the relationship from a 1st century woman's perspective. What saves us is not our decision. What saves us is Jesus Christ who became engaged to us before we even accepted that reality.

Usually, we wake up from our spiritual sleep after repentance. We refocus our minds to accept our relationship with Jesus Christ. Then, as we walk with HIM along with the Holy Spirit, we begin to experience the fruit of salvation.

Otherwise, salvation is a business transaction. A commodity we get. If this be so then it has the weak link of a human decision. We will then always doubt our level of repentance, faith, trust, or works. Or in other words, how good is good enough.

When I first beheld salvation as a relationship and no longer a commodity is when the fruit of God became more active. The heart and mind of God was more intense within my very soul. I for one am very thankful Jesus Christ re-opened the door for us to have a relationship with Him. And along with HIM, His Father, and His Spirit: the Triune God. How about you?

#275 – Relate or Influence

"For this is the message that you have heard from the beginning, that we should love one another."
1 John 3:11

What do you seek from your relationships? Friendship? Love? Intimacy? Or are people to be used for your personal agenda?

The older I become the more thankful I am for the friends and family in my world. What I realize now more than ever is that I didn't go about asking them to change for me nor I for them. Instead, we accept each other as who we are and learn to appreciate each other as God created and gifted us. Whereas in those early years, I made the immature mistake of wanting to change others. The focus was on influencing them by whatever means at my disposal. My goal wasn't to build a mutual, beneficial, unconditional relationship. But to do my agenda for the day.

Isn't that how many of us relate with others? We either accept them for who they are or we try to influence them to change. That includes our children, parents, siblings, and yes our mates.

The other day I overheard a young woman who was recently married. She stated there are a few things she is going to change about him. Otherwise, they are not going to have a successful marriage. It brought back memories of my early married days. When there were certain habits my wife had (and still has) that I was going to change. Likewise, she would admit that there were many habits that I had (and still have) that she was going to change. Thankfully, we learned early enough one can't change the other person. It cannot happen from the outside-in. Instead we first focused on building up the relationship. We

64

didn't try to persuade the other person to our point of view. Instead, we waited for God to work from the inside-out to make changes in the other.

Think about your relationships. Is the goal to mutually enjoy the love, friendship and even the intimacy of marriage? Or is the goal to influence the other person to change for your sake?

I am always amazed at how Jesus related with other people. Have you ever noticed His tenancy was to first relate with people? He actually took the time to love them and respect them for who they were. When verbally attacked, HE would defend himself with the appropriate answer. The only time HE emotionally exploded was in the temple with the money changers. And again with the self-righteous religious leaders. They always tried to trap him. (Even then it could be debated that HE was practicing tough love techniques). Otherwise, HE spent his time solving people's problems. He healed them. He ate with them. He partied with them. And as a rabbi, HE taught them.

His primary focus was to first love the people wherever HE went. His influence came later through the people who HE invested time with during his 3 1/2 year ministry. His influence was a byproduct of his relationship. He loved first; and then let his love be the influence that transformed lives in and through others. Isn't that a good plan for all to follow?

#276 – Being Fully Human

"Therefore, if anyone is in Christ, he is a new creation. The old has passed away; behold, the new has come." 2 Corinthians 5:17

In the Book of Genesis, we discover that God made man in His image after His likeness (Gen.1:26). In Psalm 8:4, King David asked the question "what is man that you are mindful of him, and the son of man that you care for him?" The writer of Hebrews in 2:6 likewise refers to the same question and adds more thought behind the remark. In 2 Corinthians 5:17, Paul writes that life in Christ makes us a new creation.

What does this all mean for you and me?

There are times when I look at our culture, I cry. My heart hurts for the people who don't really understand what Jesus means in their everyday life. For example, people may know about Him, the Cross and Resurrection. But they may not realize the importance of the Ascension and the Incarnation.

The fact is Jesus ascended into Heaven not only as a divine being but also as a resurrected human. As a human, he experienced the entire spectrum of life. He had the same emotional, psychological, and physical stress every person deals with. More so, hanging on the cross even brought greater weight into the matter. He took the sins of every person past, present, and future into his inner humanity. He knows what it means to be human. He experienced the pain of sin without ever committing sin himself (Heb.4:15).

Our connection with Father God is through Jesus Christ. Jesus' union with Father God is because of his divinity. His union with humanity is because of his bodily life. Mankind has union with Jesus because of His humanity. When we pray to our Father God, Jesus intercedes on our behalf. When we pray not knowing how and what to say, His Spirit intercedes for us (Romans 8:26-7). He is our High Priest.

He is more involved in yours and my life than you and I may ever realize. He cares about you in ways you haven't even considered yet. He wants what is best for you. He knows what it means to be human. He is our standard for what it means to be human.

He wants you to experience the same love, joy, and hope he carried with him when he walked the earth. He wants you to grow and experience the same thrills he does. Jesus wants to hang-out with you.

When Father/Son/Spirit created the world, earth, and mankind, he said it was "very good." He wants us to experience the same sense of accomplishment through our work. When Jesus healed the sick, he experienced the power of God changing people's lives. He wants us to experience the same when we serve others. When Jesus ascended into heaven, he became the first fruit of a new creation. The merger of humanity with divinity. The physical merging with the spiritual. The future new heaven and new earth being lived in the present. Heaven on earth.

Being fully human is really living and experiencing everyday life in Christ.

#277 – Separation

"For I am sure that neither death nor life, nor angels nor rulers, nor things present nor things to come, nor powers, nor height nor depth, nor anything else in all creation, will be able to separate us from the love of God in Christ Jesus our Lord." Romans 8:38-8

People remark that I sometimes may confuse the issue. Why? Because of little details that don't tie up all the loose ends. For example, the concept of sin and separation from God.

I grew up believing when I sinned God was angry at me. That sin was repulsive to God. That He would turn His back to me. That sin prevented God from blessing me. In some ways, it seemed that Sin was bigger than God. That God didn't want to have anything to do with me when I sinned. Even when we are not being aware of it. Somewhere, someplace I was erroneously led to believe I was the problem of sin. That when I sinned, God separated Himself from me.

It now amazes me more than ever what happens when the truth becomes known. For example, Father/Son/Spirit God is greater than any sin ever committed or known on planet earth. Jesus, who represents God on earth for humanity to witness, walked among sinners. He worked, played, and ate with sinners. He deliberately spent time with them. He didn't separate himself from sinners. Instead he conquered sin for us.

When we sin, God doesn't walk away from us. He doesn't turn his back to us. Instead, he pursues us even more so. He knows the ramifications of sin. He seen it with Satan. Yet He still allowed Satan to hang around heaven (Job 1:6). When Adam and Eve sinned, He didn't walk away from them. Instead he came looking for them. It was they who hid from God. It was they who became afraid and sought to hide from God.

When we sin, we hurt ourselves. We hurt those around us. Our mates, children, parents, friends, and associates all are recipients of sin's poison. God doesn't turn away from us. Those around us may, but God doesn't. He wants us to realize his forgiveness. And because of his forgiveness, he wants us to repent. He wants us to be thankful for what He does for us. Showering us with constant grace and care.

Take for example the nation of Israel. Whenever they fell into the practice of idolatry, God patiently waited. When the proper moment came, HE would intercede. He would bring the nation back into the fold. Whenever we sin, God likewise waits for us to repent before he intercedes and brings us back to him.

But HE always remains with you in the process. He wants us to always lean on HIM.

Another example. King David committed adultery and murder. God used the prophet Nathan to bring the sin to his attention. When realizing his sin, David repented. God didn't disown David. Instead, He helped David to grow in maturity and responsibility. He does the same for you and me today.

Sin doesn't separate us from God. It blinds us from seeing God. It may block God's Spirit from freely flowing through us. But God is always there. He loves us. Wants what is best for us. In some ways, He uses sin to help us appreciate and grow in his grace.

Like King David, when we are convicted of sin, we repent. In repentance, we are thankful for the life He shares with us. We are thankful for His grace, His mercy, and everything else HE has reserved for us. We are also thankful HE continues to allow us to share our life with HIM.

#278 – Theology 101

"All Scripture is breathed out by God and profitable for teaching, for reproof, for correction, and for training in righteousness..." 2 Timothy 3:9

Why is theology important?

Recently we had a lively discussion about the importance of theology. The majority of the group believed that the Bible was all that they needed. That theology was man's attempt to lead people astray. They looked at the Bible through the eyes of one simple worldview. They admitted all they knew was what they initially learned in Sunday School. They didn't care to understand why their denominational brothers and sisters believed otherwise. As far as they were concern, what they believed was right and others were wrong. They didn't realize that everyone already has a theological belief. The question is "what is yours?"

First, theology is simply the study of God. It studies the Bible from a wholesome point of view. Instead of extracting pieces of the Word at a time, it looks to bring all the pieces together. The purpose is to form a coherent understanding of God's hand in the matter.

There is a study of God for a multitude of different subjects. For example, there is the theology of salvation. The theology of grace. The theology of creation. The theology of the Kingdom of God. The theology of (add whatever subject comes to mind). There is most likely already a study on the matter.

The thought that what one believes may not be correct bothers some people. The idea that others may have more truth on a subject matter may also be humbling for a few. The relevancy of any theological belief is the Christ-like fruit it bears. If love, joy, and peace is the mainstay of a person's life, then one may want to listen and learn. We all have a theological belief system in play. The question comes to how close is the study to reality and truth. Of course reality and truth is measured through one person: Jesus Christ. And yes there is a theology of Christ, called Christology.

The more we come to know and understand God, the more we are humbled. We are at awe of His divine work and physical masterpiece. The better we understand the beliefs of others, the easier it becomes to communicate. This is why theology is important. Good theology grounds us in Christ. Our journey through life becomes more immeasurable with gratitude, love, and joy.

I may not agree with others theological position at times, but I do love and respect them. My heart understands that whoever may be closer to the truth, God in His time will reveal that to us too. The important thing is to continue grow in the grace and knowledge of Jesus Christ. That is a simple theological position every mature believer I meet agrees too. And so do I.

#279 - Beaten, Busted, Broken

"For the thing that I fear comes upon me, and what I dread befalls me. I am not at ease, nor am I quiet; I have no rest, but trouble comes." Job: 3:25-26

Life has a tendency to throw us lemons. Those who are positive thinkers, state that we need to transform the lemons into lemonade. Yet what about us who are not equipped to make it happen? Not everyone has the talent or character to pick up one self and rise up to the occasion. Or this time the challenge is larger than anything we have faced before and we don't know where to turn to. Now what?

At times like this I am comforted by God's reply to Job's challenge. Job was the wealthiest person in his neck of the woods. He had a large family and was known throughout the community for his philanthropic work. He was the picture of success. Even God claimed He was blameless.

Yet bad things do happen to good people. In Job's case, he was the pawn in a wager between God and Satan. God gave Satan authority to do whatever he wanted but spare his life. So with his walking papers, Satan destroyed Job's business, family, and health. By the time Satan was done, Job was beaten, busted, and broken.

He was physically disabled with chronic pain. He was financially ruined. His wife deserted him. His immediate family taken away. He was left alone beaten, busted, and broken. Yet he never disowned His God. In fact, he spent the time seeking answers from God. His three companions tried to comfort him. But ended up throwing spiritual daggers into his side. As the events unfolded, God finally granted him his day in court. Afterward, Job repented from his thinking and acknowledged God's greatness and faithfulness.

God restored Job with more at the end of his crisis than before his broken, busted, and beaten state. What is it that I find encouraging about the entire ordeal?

Simply that God was always with him. Even when God wages a bet with others, he does so knowing the final outcome is going to be better than if He did nothing. For most of us, we will experience a Good Friday event in our life. But, if we hang in there long enough, we will also experience a Resurrection Sunday.

God is good. He wants what is best for us all. The immediate future may look bleak. But God in all his glory will carry us through the situation and bless us with character, virtue, and reward.

Yes we may be beaten, busted, and broken now. But it only allows us to place our trust in the hand of who will rise us up and restore us to a place for his glory. With Job, his story has become an inspiration for millions throughout history. For us, our story may likewise become a living testament for others on the grace of God.

Again, being beaten, busted, and broken isn't bad unless we neglect to lean on Him. Then pity on us. I choose to trust Him who raises the dead, walks on water, and turns water into wine.

There is a purpose and meaning behind the BBB of life. We learn from it. We grow from it. We glorify God through it. In hindsight, we may have a better understanding of why we went through it. But for today, let's search-out how He will intervene. How HE will save us from ourselves, for the sake of others, and for His glory. Trouble comes; but HE is always with us through the entire ordeal.

#280 – Who Before What or What Before Who?

"...knowledge puffs up, but love builds up." 1 Corinthians 8:1

One lesson we all eventually learn is when we inappropriately place the "what" before the "who."

When reading about the life of Jesus, I am always intrigued with HIS discussions. Especially with the religious teachers. When their intent was to trap him in His interpretation of the law. Or when their self-righteous attitude blinded them in their misunderstanding of the law. Then again, maybe I read more into the narrative than what is revealed. But the teachers debating with Jesus seem to place greater emphasis on the "what." They emphasize the information/knowledge. But Jesus always seemed to focus first on the "who". A loving relationship with the person before adding the "what".

For example, when seeking truth most of us seek information. Yet God teaches that Truth is personified in Jesus Christ. From the central core of Jesus, all other truths prevail. The who comes before the what.

Jesus once was presented with a women caught in adultery. The accusers wanted him to agree with their interpretation of the Law. (Most likely these were religious people who place the "what" above the "who"). Jesus, in his graceful and impactful manner began to scribble words in the sand. By the time he stopped, all the accusers fled. Jesus than forgave her sins and extended mercy to a fellow human being. He placed the who before the what.

Now the "what" is important. Knowledge leads to understanding and wisdom. But knowledge without relationship leads to legalistic, emotional

74

brutality. Thus, as Jesus demonstrated, the "who" takes precedence over the "what."

So the next time you feel like pontificating what you know, stop. Instead, emphasize the "who." In other words, let love lead. For from love, the "what" is more easily presented. From love, the "who" is honored and respected. From the basis of love, everything else falls into place. Yes, the "what" may be important, but the "who" is always more important.

#281 - Living in God's Presence

"...And behold, I (Jesus) am with you always, to the end of the age." Matthew 28:20

Want to take part in the greatest adventure of life? Want an accountability partner that understands you? Want to be held accountable to a higher standard? If so, than live in the presence of God.

The other day, the worship leader invited God into the church service. My thought was "isn't He here already?"

The preacher stands on the corner holding his end of the world sign. He is shouting, "God wants nothing to do with you until you repent." Which begs the question: Than why does God provide rain and sunshine to the unjust like He does to the just?

After a very profitable year, the business owner asks the pastor. "How much do I need to donate to the church to keep receiving God's blessings?" Which leads to another question. Is his relationship with God built on a contractual arrangement? Or a grace-filled, loving Father connection?

When one begins to understand the good news of Jesus Christ, one relishes the joy of living in His Presence. When you deny the self. When you carry your personal cross. When you follow Jesus wherever He leads you. When we do, the world begins to look differently.

When you realize Jesus Christ already justified every person, Kingdom values take over. So as we meet people, we prayerfully seek to discover how the Spirit is working with the person. We seek ways to love the person as Christ loves us; through service. Our aim is to witness Jesus to the person without words. To allow the Spirit to convict and introduce the person to the savior of the world.

As we enter the marketplace, we seek to take part with Jesus in the work we do. We strive to balance excellence with love as a witness of God's Kingdom economy. In everything we do, we acknowledge Him. We pray. We ask, seek, and knock for solutions in business and relationships. We judge no one; not even ourselves. We live accountable to Jesus.

When wrong, HE will discipline us. When right, HE will help us to keep humble as we know it all comes from Him. Where we lack faith, we will rely on HIS. When love flickers, we ask Him to intercede. When walking, bicycling, or driving, we communicate with Him. We seek ways to bring glory to Him. As we place our trust in Him, he reveals Himself through the people and means that come our way. We become more aware of His work in the world. We seek ways to take part with His purposes. Whenever we fail, HE is there to carry us through to the very end.

He is always with us. He is always available and nearer to you than you and I even realize. Be glad. It is an honor to live in His presence each day.

#282 – Preach What?

"But when they believed Philip as he preached good news about the kingdom of God and the name of Jesus Christ, they were baptized, both men and women." Acts 8:12

The other day a pastor on TV emphasized that He preaches the Bible. Another preacher on the other station states that he preaches Jesus Christ. It raised the question. Which is the message of the Kingdom? The Bible or Jesus Christ?

Whenever one elevates the Bible or equates the written Word with the personal Word, my historical journey flashes before me. Danger flags are now waved. It begs the question; how do you interpret the Bible? What is the basis of your preaching? Is the main thing the Bible or who the Bible points to?

When a person preaches Jesus Christ as Savior, Messiah, and Lord, the focus is on the main thing - Jesus. The Bible introduces the reader to Jesus. The Incarnate Jesus reveals Father God to us. As we read and study the life, work, and heart of Jesus, we learn more about God. As we grow in the grace and knowledge of Jesus, we learn to follow in his steps. As we study the Bible through a Jesus-centered Triune God worldview, we secure a more solid basis of interpreting Scripture.

Our focus is to build a stronger relationship with the eternal God. The Bible is simply a means to this end.

Our partnership and participation is with Jesus; not the Bible. He is redeeming humanity; not the Bible. Our job is to abide and follow Him. To listen to His word as He communicates to us. The Bible serves as a means for God to communicate to us through His Spirit. As we read and study the inspired Word, we are open to hear his voice. As we learn to hear his voice, we are more attuned to recognize Him during the activities of the day. It is His Spirit that inspires us, encourages us, and opens us up to serve those around us.

Again, the Bible is the means, not the message. The message is Jesus Christ, His Spirit, and His Domain. Secondary, but including within that message is how we take part with HIM through the sanctification phase.

Jesus is the reason we have the Bible. So, if the preaching is not centered around Jesus Christ, be careful. If the message doesn't explain how Jesus is the foundation of your growth, service, and faith, be on guard. If the emphasis is on what you need to do and not what Jesus has done, is doing, and will do, be suspect. Remember, Jesus came with good news; not more burdens, yokes, and hurdles for you to climb.

#283 – Tweet Gospel

"...there are some who trouble you and want to distort the gospel of Christ." Galatians 1:7

Twitter is one of those modern techno gadgets that I haven't had time nor desire to take on at this season of life. My understanding is one communicates using abbreviations and special codes. The entire sentence is limited to approximately 120 letters/numbers/characters. Since I have a difficult time communicating with 400 words via a blog, it will be a while before I attempt to tweet.

There is a time for abbreviations. But not with the message of Jesus Christ. When we share the gospel through technology, could the Good News be short-changed? Just like a tweet. Instead of sharing the entire message of Jesus Christ, we only share one aspect of it. Usually that aspect is the forgiveness of sin. Though it is one reason that Jesus broke time and space as a human person, it is only one reason. And in my opinion, it isn't the main reason.

For example, when one reads the four gospel accounts of Jesus. His message wasn't solely about the forgiveness of sin. He introduced himself as the King of a government - The Kingdom of God. Some theologians like to only speak about the kingdom in our hearts. They forget the Kingdom He spoke about was the fulfillment of the Messiah prophecies. Also the universal order that included heaven and earth. Kingdom reality is already here. There are those who are participating with Him now. They are partnering with Him in His work to restore creation back to His original intent.

Besides, when one reads the letters of Paul, one is introduced to God's plan from the beginning of creation. There he states we are included in the adoption of humanity into the inner circle of the Triune God (Eph. 1:4). Before man was created and sinned, God already had a plan in motion. Sin and the forgiveness of sin was only a messy inkblot in His plan for the universe. His initial purpose was not to save us, but to adopt us into His world.

When we repent (change our mind of who God is and what He is doing) God impregnates us with his Spirit. As we abide in Christ, our values change. As we take up our cross, we learn responsibility. As we follow Him, HE mentors us. As the Spirit changes our hearts and minds, our character and attitude reflects HIM (2 Timothy 1:7). The Holy Spirit of God begins to remove the darkness of sin from our life. The addictions, lies, self-righteousness, pride of life, vanity, anger, hatred is being replaced. With what? The fruit of the Holy Spirit and the virtues of God.

There is also the good news of grace, freedom, justice, and resurrection. In other words, it is far more than being saved from our sins and acquiring a one way ticket to heaven. It's about people flourishing with other people within God's governmental order. It's about being adopted into a royal and ministering family that rules the universe. And yes, it's about transformation. Being prepared and equipped with the character of God to serve others and God now and for eternity.

The good news of Jesus Christ is truly more than what we hear, know or imagine.

#284 – Sin or Adoption

"The next day he saw Jesus coming toward him, and said, "Behold, the Lamb of God, who takes away the sin of the world!" John 1:29

"... In love he predestined us for adoption as sons through Jesus Christ, according to the purpose of his will,..." Ephesians 1:4-5

When one reads the Bible, what is the general premise of one's viewpoint? We all read the Bible with preconceived ideas and concepts. They are generally what we have been told, read somewhere, or blindsided by peoples bias. The result is many of us grew up in a Christian culture with a worldview based on the premise of either Sin or Adoption.

For example, many people read the Bible with the premise Jesus' came to earth solely to take away our sins. If they accept Christ into their life, personal sins are forgiven and heaven is the reward. The entire process seems to follow a contractual transaction between God and man. So, when they read the Bible, sin is the fundamental basis of one's belief. Their emphasis than is built around what one must personally do to manage the process of sin.

Now there are those who read the Bible on the premise Jesus came to adopt humanity into the family of the Triune God. Christ's vicarious life, death, resurrection, and ascension paved the way for us. Before we even knew Him. Before we even asked for forgiveness. Before we even believed in Jesus as our Savior, Messiah, and Lord. This premise places more emphasis on the familial relationship of the Triune God. That the salvation process is built on what Jesus did, is doing, and will do.

Both premises speak about Sin and Relationship. But each emphasizes the one over the other. I have come to lean more towards salvation as explained through Adoption theology. It aligns more with who HE IS and HIS purpose for life. For I have come to know HIM as a relational God. One who unconditionally loves, is passionately faithful, and exercises justice and grace. HE is able to fulfill His vision for humanity through the Incarnate work of Jesus Christ. Sin is only an ink blot that made the process more messier. Adoption was the goal from the very beginning of time.

#285 - Christian Crutches

"As for the one who is weak in faith, welcome him, but not to quarrel over opinions." Romans 14:1

One of the most puzzling aspects of the Christian faith is the various denominations. So many are built around a specific interpretation of Scripture. Last time I looked there are over 30,000 different denominations in the United States alone. These of course include non-denominational organizations. Each one operates as a single-body denomination.

These faith communities may place unique emphasize on a specific doctrine. Could be how they interpret communion. Ways to practice baptism. The importance of prophecy. Defining the gospel message. Is there healing today? Does the Gospel also include a prosperity message? etc... But still the vast majority believe Jesus Christ is Savior and Lord. Thus, according to Scripture, they are my brothers and sisters in the Lord. The challenge is their strong preference and opinion. In some circles, they follow the formula that to be a Christian requires Jesus plus "x". The emphasis placed on the "x" factor separates them from others.

What they may not see is that this "x" factor is a spiritual crutch they currently need. Yet one day the Holy Spirit will complete His transformation within the Believer. Then they will realize the crutch was only a temporary band-aid. Meanwhile, the crutch helps them in their walk with the Lord. The problem is they sincerely believe everyone else should have the same crutch.

Most transformational processes take considerable time. Yet upon completion, one only then recognizes the crutch of the matter.(sorry for the pun).

In Jesus' time on earth, he kept correcting the religious leaders of his day. They would emphasize the importance of the crutch. Meanwhile Jesus was healing the person so they wouldn't need the crutch any longer. It is not a shame to have a crutch. It is a means that allows us to continue walking with Christ until we are healed in that area of life. Until that day, we aspire for unity in all essentials beliefs. (Jesus Christ is Lord and Savior). We encourage liberty in beliefs which are gray or uncertain. (interpretation of scripture, baptism, end-times, etc.). But exercise love in all beliefs.

Remember, we all use crutches. We all will walk with a limp into the fullness of the Kingdom of God. So, let's just recognize what is a crutch. Than continue to abide in Jesus Christ. Allow God's Spirit to transform the heart, mind, and soul for His glory and purpose. Plus mutually serve one another through the maturity growth process.

Crutch or no crutch, I for one am thankful that Jesus is the one we all have to answer too.

#286 - Let Christ Lead

"So faith comes from hearing, and hearing through the word of Christ." Romans 10:17

One of the traditions on January 1st is to establish a new goal for the coming year.

If you are one who makes such commitments, how about making one with God? Specifically, a covenant to focus more attention on hearing the word of God. No, I'm not saying spend more time reading the Word (though that wouldn't hurt). Nor listening to more preaching (that always helps). But to actually spend time listening for God's influence in your life.

One reason we read the Bible is to gain knowledge of God's Word. But knowledge doesn't build faith. Hearing the Word builds the faith we need. Otherwise, if God speaks to us, how do we know it is Him?

By reading the Word, we gather a basic understanding of who God is. We study the life and relationship between Jesus, His Father, and the Holy Spirit. We pray to communicate with our heavenly Father. Though we may not know what to say, we are assured Jesus intercedes on our behalf. In most cases with the appropriate request.

Have you ever wondered how a sermon is received by listeners with different messages? When you ask the congregation , they will give you a multitude of various answers? Isn't it amazing how the Spirit works through the words spoken by the minister making it personal for each of us.

Have you ever prayed seeking an answer from God and the reply came from the most unusual place? How often the answer you seek comes through a person at the checkout counter at the grocery store? Confirmed by the officer who pulled you over for speeding the same day? And reconfirmed by your child at the dinner table? God speaks to us in many different ways. This is why it helps to know His Word. To value His Character. And appreciate His method of operations. When you do, you become more aware of His influence in your life. For some it may be a word. For others in may be a nudge. For some it may be an inspiration. Others it may be like a rainbow in the sky. For each of us grasp information in different ways. Doesn't God know the best way to communicate with us?

How about this year focusing on one thing in regards to the Lord? How about listening to Jesus Christ who lives in you and allow Him to lead you in every avenue of your life? Forget the rules. Gain knowledge of His Word and then listen for him to show you how it applies in your entire life. That includes your marriage, your parenting, your business, and your community service. Invite Him into everything you do. Let Him lead you. You may be surprised with the results.

#287 - Learning to Govern

God blessed them; and God said to them, "Be fruitful and multiply, and fill the earth, and subdue it; and rule over the fish of the sea and over the birds of the; sky and over every living thing that moves on the earth." Genesis 1:28 (NASB)

There is one theme which moves through the entire Bible that caught my attention this week. One characteristic God wants humanity to learn while stationed on this planet. It started in Genesis where God instructs man and woman to rule the earth's infrastructure. Then reiterated in Revelation 5:10 where John writes about Jesus' end game. He recognizes the saints in this life are being led to govern. To learn how to best lead and serve in God's Kingdom. Could this be one of God's purposes for you and I in this life? To learn how to best govern.

He initially placed Adam and Eve in a garden to manage it. He built a family unit starting with Abraham, Isaac, and Jacob. The family unit became a tribe and then the nation of Israel. During this time, HE trained specific individuals for leadership position. Joseph, second in rank behind Pharaoh. Daniel, a president under the Babylonian system. David and Solomon, kings of Israel. There are many others – good leaders and bad rulers.

He designed the family unit where parents learn to govern their households. Children learn to follow and develop their personal governing skills. He led people to build institutions. Business, education, medical, legal, entertainment, and yes governments. Each institution allows us to learn how to work with others to help a community to flourish. He also built the Church. A community of believers united within Himself.

All these opportunities are simply a shadow to prepare you and I to govern within the Kingdom of God. God's Kingdom is the Triune God's family business. You and I as his children have been given the opportunity now to learn. To learn how to best govern the self and others for this purpose. We allow the Holy Spirit to work within us renovating our hearts to see and hear as our Triune God sees and hears. We govern with love and purpose. We allow righteousness to flourish and evil to diminish. We serve our King bringing Him honor and respect and glory.

God has bigger plans for you and I than we will ever phantom on this side of heaven. For now, He gives us a small taste of His divine presence. HE fills our heart with joy as we learn to govern His way for His people for His glory.

Life is a learning process preparing you and I for eternity. Run with it!!

#288 - Savior, Messiah, King

"She will bear a son, and you shall call his name Jesus, for he will save his people from their sins."
Matthew 1:21

*"He will be great and will be called the Son of the Most High. And the Lord God will give to him
the throne of his father David, and he will reign over the house of Jacob forever, and of his
kingdom there will be no end." Luke 1:32-33*

"We have found the Messiah" (which means Christ)" John 1:41

What is Christmas all about?

Is it a national holiday? Is it a religious holy day? Is it a birthday celebration?

What does the exchange of presents have to do with Christmas? Is it a day we give ourselves a license to buy the things we always wanted but could never justify? Is it group mentality gone array?

Big business manipulates the airwaves with advertisement. Nonprofits increase their fund development campaigns. The western world gives itself an excuse to party hard. Is it all really about Jesus or something else? What is the reason for the season?

I use too and still do become angry during Christmas season. The commercialism and self-indulgence showcases itself each year blinding us from knowing Jesus. I also laugh realizing historically this season of the year was once a pagan celebration. But Christians redeemed it for Christ. (We may still be trying to figure out how to live-out the redemption part.) Yet, I am glad that

Jesus is given some recognition in the public media and national channels. I only wish it was more.

I find it interesting that Jesus never asked us to celebrate his birth. We don't even know the date of His birth. But we do know that He is no longer a baby. He sits on a throne in heaven intervening for you and me. He is humanity's Savior, Israel's Messiah, and Heaven & Earth's King. He is the reason for this and every season!

So this Christmas, and every Christmas, and every day between, let's Celebrate Him! Let's thank Him for what He has done, is doing, and will do. For He is the reason for all our seasons.

#289 – Feelings

"A fool gives full vent to his spirit, but a wise man quietly holds it back." Proverbs 29:11

"I don't feel like it!"

How often have we expressed the same?

What did we do with that feeling?

Did we follow through as a victim of our feelings?

Or did we balance the feelings with God's Character?

Did we weigh the feeling with His Word?

What is the truth when you compare your feelings with His Word?

Yes, there are times when our feelings will be correct. Other times your feelings will blind you to the truth.

Be a wise person. Stop, pull back, and evaluate the situation. Don't let your feelings lead you. Instead, allow the foundation of God's love, grace, and truth be your guide.

#290 - "You Are Invited"

"Come, follow me, Jesus said..." Mark 1:7

It all begins with God. He created the world which included humanity. He planned, designed, and executed a God-size strategy. He opened the door for His creation to join Him in His journey.

He invited Abraham, Isaac, and Jacob to join Him. He invited the entire nation of Israel to join Him. Through Jesus, he invited the entire remaining human race to join Him.

He doesn't force, coerce, or manipulate you to join Him. He doesn't threaten you, remove His common grace, or strike you with lighting if you don't join Him.

He has given you the free choice to follow Him or not. He respects you as a person. He doesn't interfere with your plans unless he is invited. This is why I appreciate the prayers of my parents, family members, friends, and fellow saints on my behalf. Their prayers invites God to intervene in my life. There I am able to accept His invitation willingly and joyfully within my personal space.

Is it interesting how the mature invites the novice to take part in something that will benefit them? The mentor who invites the mentees to learn from her. The trader who invites others to join him and learn how to successfully trade the markets. The teacher inviting the student to a specific field of study built upon their strengths. The carpenter who hires an apprentice to learn the business. We see it all around us.

Isn't evangelism inviting others into a relationship with the living God? They can choose to join or not. It is their choice. The best we can do is invite them, pray for them, and love them on behalf of Jesus Christ. He invites us into a personal relationship with Him. Can't we do the same for others?

#291 – Fiat Character

"Not only that, but we rejoice in our sufferings, knowing that suffering produces endurance, and endurance produces character, and character produces hope,and hope does not put us to shame, because God's love has been poured into our hearts through the Holy Spirit who has been given to us." Romans 3:3-5

Wouldn't it be great if our character could be molded and built overnight? Instead, we have to discipline our thoughts, attitudes, and habits for years. Why couldn't we take a pill and have instant Godly character? We know that is not reality. So if someone offers you such a "pill" or shortcut, beware. Only God's love and grace is there for us to experience the downside of character building.

When God created man and women, He did so after his image and likeness (Gn. 1:26). Of all creation, only humanity has the ability to reason, imagine, and create. These characteristics are patterned after God's likeness. Yet man also, because of the sin virus, is blacken with spiritual cancer. He needs healing. That healing comes to us via Jesus Christ. He sends the Holy Spirit into our lives to heal and restore our hearts and minds. Our participation involves building our Will through the choices we make. It requires obedience. Most often it requires obedience through the tough difficult times of life. Even Jesus learned through what he suffered (Hebrews 5:8).

Paul writes that the purpose of life is for us to grow into the image of Jesus Christ (Eph. 4:24). When the Bible speaks about image it doesn't mean that everyone looks like Him. What it means is that we resemble His character and spirit. That character and spirit comes through the trials and tests that life presents. It doesn't come via a pill. It doesn't come by taking a class. It doesn't come by joining a church. It only comes when we allow His Spirit to lead us, transform us, and walk with us through the challenges of life.

So forget about fiat character. Instead, learn to walk with the Triune God as He restores creation back to His original intent. That includes you, me, and all creation.

Perseverance. Endurance. Faithfulness. They are not the glorious words in a self-esteemed society. Yet they are the marathon characteristics of a "little Christ" in today's world.

#292 - Poor in Spirit

"Blessed are the poor in spirit, for theirs is the kingdom of heaven." Matthew 5:3

Who are the poor in spirit? Are we not taught to be rich in spirit? Is not those who have a positive attitude the ideal standard? Are not those with an assurance of confidence and strong self-esteem the model to desire? Are these not the spirits we are told will make us happy? Did Jesus get it all wrong?

Some people believe that if one is poor in material goods, than one is also poor in spirit? Others say that poor in spirit is an attitude of humility. In Revelation 3:17 the writer addresses those in the church. He writes they have the appearance of success but are living in spiritual poverty. Who then are the poor in spirit?

When one walks with the Lord, the vast difference between the teacher and student shows. One acknowledges the Teacher is the Master and the student is the pupil. When a student compares themself with the Teacher, their lack of holiness is revealed. When God's love and grace is experienced, then one begins to realize how far below the measuring bar one sits.

One soon begins to pray and ask God for the fruit of His Spirit to grow within themselves. Yet even as the fruit begins to bloom in one's life, one is always comparing themselves with Jesus. In that regard, how vastly poor are we compared with the vast riches found in Christ.

When one compares themselves with their neighbor, one is spiritually immature. It is easy to think one has arrived to the highest level of spiritual maturity when compared to the devil. Yet when one compares themselves with Jesus Christ, one admits their state of poverty. It is only through the Spirit of

Christ that one inherits the richness of His Kingdom. It is only through Christ, that one experiences the treasurers of the Kingdom of God.

Yes, one needs to admit how poor they are without Christ. And yes to acknowledge our neediness for Christ. When one repents and begins to follow HIM, then begins the experience of Kingdom living. It all begins when one realizes how poor they are when compared with the Incarnate God.

#293 - Inherit The Earth

"Blessed are the meek, for they shall inherit the earth." Matthew 5:5

How in the world are the meek going to inherit the earth? In our current system of governments, is not the strong and powerful who conquer lands? If you put a meek person up against a strong man, what is our perception on who is going to win the fight? So how does the meek inherit the earth?

To better understand the how, one needs to know the goal of salvation. The aim of salvation isn't just to receive a ticket for eternal life. It involves so much more. God's goal is to restore creation back to his original intent. Eventually history leads to the climatic achievement. The time when a new heaven and earth is merged together as one new creation. (Revelation 21-22). All this proposed before the foundation of the world. Then implemented through the new birth of Jesus Christ via a resurrection.

The resurrection of Jesus began the new birth of a new humanity. This new creation involves the merging of the physical and spiritual. As Jesus was 100% human and 100% divine, he paved the way for others to follow him. When we accept His authority in our life, he births us with a new Spirit. This spirit is the Holy Spirit that opens the way for us to have an adopted relationship with the living God.

Now as children of God, with our hearts being soften by the Spirit, the fruit of that Spirit becomes our DNA. Included within that DNA is the spirit of gentleness. In some Bible versions this is translated as meekness. So when Jesus said that those who are meek will inherit the earth, he is casting the vision of the end time. He is highlighting the reward for those who follow him. Now we are being trained as kings and priests of his domain (Rev 1:6, 5:10, 20:6). Meanwhile, our inheritance is stored in heaven until the culmination of all things (Eph 1:10).

So yes the meek will inherit the earth. Not because of our strength, smarts, or spirituality. But only because of Jesus Christ.

#294 - Why Read The Bible?

"Therefore, as you received Christ Jesus the Lord, so walk in him, rooted and built up in him and established in the faith, just as you were taught, abounding in thanksgiving." Colossians 2:6-7

When you want to learn about someone, what do you do? Don't we search the Internet and see what we can find out. Don't we ask people who may personally know the person? Maybe we may eventually schedule a visit and spend time with the person.

So why read the Bible? Here are some practical, everyday what-if questions that point to the Bible.

* What if you had the means to develop a more intimate relationship with the Living God? To find out more about Him? His heart? His mind? His character?

* What if you could better understand His work on earth and heaven?

* What if you could learn ways to unleash His authority to impact your world today?

* What if you could explore and integrate the impact of heavenly virtue into your micro world?

* What if you could learn to transfer heavenly treasurers into everyday life?

* What if you could stop making the same mistakes others have made? Isn't it smarter to learn from the successes and failures of others?

* What if you had a venue to listen for the Holy Spirit interpret God's Will personally for you?

* What if you had a streaming source of life-giving wisdom for every season of life?

* What if you had your own personal success guide written for you?

You would have insight of the best practices for life. The best finance tips. A marriage planner. Proven family instructions. Profit laden business practices. All proven over millenniums of time.

* What if you had a guide revealing how God interrelates with humanity? And also how you could better interrelate with Him?

* What if you could more easily identify the Truth and its implications within reality?

* What if you had a written script to help you better understand your purpose in life?

The Bible expresses the love, grace, and authority of Jesus Christ. If you want to serve the King of Kings, don't you think it would help you to better understand His macro purpose and plans? Also to support His methods and means of working with you and others? What if you spent a few more minutes each day discovering more about the Triune God? What difference do you think it would make in your world? It may not be a radical idea, but its implementation certainly is.

#295 - Turning The World Upside Down

"This Jesus, whom I proclaim to you, is the Christ." And some of them were persuaded and joined Paul and Silas, as did a great many of the devout Greeks and not a few of the leading women. But the Jews were jealous, and taking some wicked men of the rabble, they formed a mob, set the city in an uproar, and attacked the house of Jason, seeking to bring them out to the crowd. And when they could not find them, they dragged Jason and some of the brothers before the city authorities, shouting, "These men who have turned the world upside down have come here also, and Jason has received them, and they are all acting against the decrees of Caesar, saying that there is another king, Jesus." Acts 17:3-7

Have you ever noticed to become successful in today's world, there are times you have to go opposite of the norm? Eventually one learns worldly standards enslaves you to your self-defeating passions. But Godly morals produce freedom, flourishment, and virtuous growth for you and others. For many people, the Christ-centered life is the opposite of how they have been educated. So, when the world looks at Kingdom living, they focus on what they are going to personally lose. Jesus apprentices look at what they and others will gain.

The world's institutions are generally built upon humanistic principles. They include the educational, governmental, judicial, commercial, and scientific functions. To espouse that Jesus is King of all these entities would be ludicrous in the eyes of many of its leaders. Yet, the early church didn't mince words. They profusely stated Jesus is King. Not only King of heaven, or the Jews, but King of all the heavens and earth! A bold statement then and still a bold statement today.

When one acknowledges that Jesus is King, one's world begins to turn upside down. But, overtime one realizes what is truly upside down is today's world.

The Messiah came to restore humanity onto a path that will end with the birth of a new Eden. Today his children are gaining knowledge and experience of this way of life in Christ. We capture a glimpse of the vision and a small taste of Kingdom living now.

Yes in the eyes of others the Christ-follower is someone strange. For they accept Jesus today as their priest and king. But in the eyes of God, we are HIS children being trained for future responsibility. HE gives Christ-followers His Spirit to transform us. His domain to encircle us. His faithfulness to encourage us. His grace to change us. We are His living examples. We show others what it means to live under Kingdom love. Kingdom freedom. Kingdom economics. Kingdom growth.

So if you think we are turning the world upside down, think again. We follow Christ as He turns the world right-side up!

#296 - God, Family, Character

"You will eat the fruit of your labor; blessings and prosperity will be yours." Psalms 128:2

Thanksgiving is one of the national holidays I enjoy. A time to give thanks to our Awesome Benefactor for the bountifulness of this great country.

To reflect on this unique country and its history makes one realize how blessed as a nation America is. To see the progressive improvements from the pilgrims first settlement to now. To see my parents legally immigrate after World War II to raise a family and have a good life. To watch illegal aliens risk their lives for entrance. All this makes one realize how special this nation has become. Yet we also cry inside as we watch this country throw out the baby with the bath water.

When you read early American historians, you note three common themes of greatness. God, Family, and Character made this country special. This God of our early history wasn't an idealistic idea, but a Providential Ruler. Thomas Jefferson was inspired to acknowledge these rights are bestowed by this Creator. This God was allowed to be involved in early governmental affairs. Today, we disavow His involvement in public affairs. The price paid is becoming more costly each year.

In the early years of American life, family was the backbone of community success. Families would need labor to operate farms. So having one dozen children was not unusual but a necessity to assist with the chores. Families learned to depend on each other for survival and entertainment. Children learned practical survival skills that included hunting, farming, and Biblical common sense. Today, we don't depend on family for such necessities of life.

As a result the nuclear family is disappearing. Likewise the favorable results families produce is dying. Instead of learning how to work-out problems between two people, we now exit the situation. We have placed our individual needs before others. Yes today's generation is labeled the most narcissistic since the keeping of records.

Of course, it took work and sacrifice to build America into an economic powerhouse. What helped is the Providential Benefactor's blessings of an idealistic land and climate. It wasn't about seeking easy street. It was about discipline, hard work, sacrifice, and willing to risk everything for a better life. Why is it families coming into this country with nothing leave an estate for their children? In some cases it rivals wealthy people around the world. They know the sacrifice and hard work required to live a dream. But today we have raised a generation who lack the character to live out the American dream.

Jesus came so we may take part with Him in His new creation. A life of plenty. A life of transformation from the Old Human to a New Human. That new Human involves the development of Godly character. The same character God employs in His eternal travels throughout the universe. His goal is for you and I to realize what it means to be human in this life and the life to come. Apart from Him though, it cannot be done.

So when you accept His authority in your life, good things begin to happen. When you allow His Spirit to lead you and influence you in your decisions and choices, good things happen. You begin to take part in a journey of transformation in Christ. Over time, through trials and tribulations, you will taste His good life now and for eternity.

That is why I am thankful this time of year. It always reminds me that no matter what is going on around, God is Good. Family is Good. Godly Character is Good. And I enjoy Good stuff.

#297 - Jesus, Merciful Judge

"And Jesus said, Neither do I condemn you; go, and from now on sin no more." John 8:11

A woman caught in the act of adultery was brought before Jesus. The people wanted Jesus to agree with the Law which stated that such a person should be stoned to death. Jesus refrained from speaking. Instead, he began to write on the ground. What he wrote we will not know this side of heaven. But as he wrote, each person from the eldest to the youngest ran away until no one was left to accuse the woman. Jesus likewise did not condemn the person. Instead he gave her a warning and a personal mission. To choose freedom and encouragement to change her ways.

When I read the last several chapters of the Book of Revelation, I am very thankful. The chapter showcases Jesus as the person who will judge us. We have a judge who has proven himself to be very merciful. And I need more mercy than most. Yet, I am also very apprehensive. Why? Because I don't always respond to Him as one fully empowered by the Holy Spirit. Yes he lives in me, leads me, and encourages me on a daily basis, but I sometimes get lazy. And yes, each season in life, we discover another area of self that is imperfect compared to our Savior.

Yep, sin is very deceptive. Most of our human difficulties are buried under the disguise of sin. We need food, clothing, and shelter to survive. So rather than trust our Maker with the solution, we seek alternative options. Instead of seeking work that is beneficial for all, we may turn to crime, prostitution, or free loafing. We want intimacy, respect, and recognition from others. So instead of having Christ fill our inner desires, we manipulate others. We try to control them. Whatever way we can bend people toward our way of thinking and goals in our natural carnal desire.

Jesus knows how strong the inner desires of an unconverted heart can become. He also knows the solution. He allows trials and tests in this life so we may mature in virtue, godliness, and Kingdom living. We can be thankful that He is our judge and jury. He knows our frame. He knows our inadequacies. He knows our fears and doubts. Yet He also knows what it is going to take to prepare us for eternity. To be a vessel that will glorify God and productive toward others.

We may be guilty for a ton of stuff that has enslaved us to this world. Yet Jesus showers us with his grace and opens the door for us to change and follow Him in His Kingdom. So like Paul before us, we don't even judge ourselves (I Corinthians 4:3). We place our trust and faith in our Merciful Judge, Jesus Christ, King of Kings and Lord of Lords. How about you?

#298 – Is God Unsafe?

"The Lord will rescue me from every evil attack and will bring me safely to his heavenly kingdom. To him be glory for ever and ever. Amen." 2 Timothy 4:18

There is a human expression that occasionally makes its appearance during tough trials. This past week I heard it again. The saying is "God is not safe; but God is good."

From a human perspective, one could shake their head in agreement. Most often this thought appears when we are blindsided from events. Instead of God preventing such occurrences, He allows them to happen. These times usually are accompanied by pain, loss, and grief. But when one begins to understand and live-out the love God has for us, HIS goodness slowly is revealed. No matter the circumstances, HIS love grows into uncompromising trust over time. The goodness of God, even in stinking times, overflows.

God is not safe for us because instead of granting our expectations, HE allows the opposite to occur. Instead of preventing bad things to happen to good people, HE allows them. HE allows good people to experience the impact of evil. So how can you trust a God who doesn't meet all your heavenly expectations when you need it most?

Because He is GOOD!

In His unsearchable character, we capture a taste of his goodness. We see it throughout his creation. Like a prudent grandparent who knows how to best present a solution to a child's problem, God knows you. HE knows what is best for you and your love ones and your community. I don't understand how, but

I've seen HIM do it over and over again in my life and in the life of others. One gains wisdom and trust with fifty plus years of hindsight.

He is unpredictable; otherwise He wouldn't be God. We at times seem to think that we know what is best for us and everyone around us. We play god and forget that there is someone who is GOD. God is good. And the perspective HE is unsafe comes when we haven't yet yielded ourselves into the Craftsman's Hand.

This life isn't meant to be permanent but a training ground for the new age tomorrow. You and I are being molded into the image of our Creator. His character is slowly being morphed into us. So one day we will stand with Jesus and serve His people with the same love, hope, and purpose as HE serves us. This is His story and you are included. Complete your part and He will fulfill his.

Evil will come against you. God may not prevent it, but HE will rescue you. And from this rescue, you will grow your trust in Him. If there was a better way, He would bring it about. But He knows what you lack and what you need. From a human perspective HE may be unsafe. But HE is a good God. Trust Him.

#299 – JOB-I-TIS

"There was a man in the land of Uz whose name was Job, and that man was blameless and upright, one who feared God and turned away from evil...this man was the greatest of all the people of the east." JOB 1:1-3

Woe is me! You are welcome to come to my self-pity party. No one understands me. Life stinks. Why doesn't God hear my prayers? I quit. These are words I and many others have said someplace, somewhere, sometime in our life. Especially when circumstances didn't meet our expectations.

At times like this, I like to reread the Book of Job in the Old Testament. Theologians believe this is the first book written in the Bible. It is a story of a very successful businessman, family man, and philanthropist. But he ran into destructive circumstances beyond his control. God even stated that Job was blameless in his walk with Him.

Yet in a manner of days, he lost everything. All his wealth, his entire family except for his wife who even doubted him, and his physical health, gone. His friends came to comfort him. But only to bombard him with religious jargon blaming him for his downfall. Most remarkably though, through the entire ordeal he remained blameless before God. His main request through this painful trial was the desire to have a conference with God. He wanted to debate his position. And God did grant him his request. In the end of his story, God confronted him and began to question Job. It was then that Job realized his insignificance before God. He acknowledged His authority. Plus appreciated coming to know Him more intimately than ever before.

Being human, we all suffer at times with what I call "JOB-I-TIS." A condition where our entire world seems to fall apart. Where we stand totally naked in mind, heart, and will before God. Where everything is beyond our capacity to manage or change. What good can come out of all this? How does one grow in the grace and knowledge of Jesus Christ? How does our relationship with the Triune God becomes more intimate?

Is it not the more challenging times when our world is collapsing that we draw closer to God? Isn't this the moment of truth when we find out where we stand before God? If our expectations are not met, we either turn to HIM or away from HIM. From there, we either return to our own ways, or we trust God that He will bring about a better solution. It is at moments like this where we are stretched beyond our self-imposed capacity. But if we hang in there long enough, we are reminded that God is doing a wonderful work in us. He is creating a new you in Christ. It isn't easy. Yet it is priceless.

Our reward may not come at this time. Or in this life. (many martyrs of the faith have displayed this fact). Yet our reward now is a more intimate, growing relationship with God. This is the byproduct of the trials and tests that life produces. To have a mutual relationship with the Creator God is more joy than one can ever imagine. And yes, even our faith is strengthen when God pulls us through the trial through the other end.

So the next time you experience that JOBITIS condition, remember Job's story. Yes he suffered through a painful event. Yet in the end, he came out more blessed than ever before. Our blessings may not be physical. But they will be good. That is the hand of God who is always with you and for you as we walk through the trials and tests of this life.

#300 – Let Your Work Worship God

"Therefore let us be grateful for receiving a kingdom that cannot be shaken, and thus let us offer to God acceptable worship, with reverence and awe..." Hebrews 12:28

When or where did today's church make a distorted turn when it comes to worship? The message that we hear so often every week is to assemble for worship. It's like the reason we assemble is to make it possible for you to worship. The implied message is that worship is something done only in church through music. (Though I'm sure this is unintentional). Again, we are instructed to gather together and praise our Lord. This is a good thing. The problem though is when we limit worship to only a church service and music. When we do, we put God into a tiny box.

The Hebrew word used throughout the Bible for worship is related with the word work. You will find the Hebrew Scriptures associate worship and work as bedfellows.

Sometimes, I think we conduct ourselves in Church opposite of God's original intentions. We generally follow the cultural thinking until we discover God's way. Take for example the Sabbath. The Hebrews kept the seventh day as a day of rest. They worked six days and rested on the seventh day. A part of their rest was attending a local synagogue. The synagogue in Christ's time were small and community-oriented. The teaching was usually an exchange between the speaker and listeners. In our post-modern Christian world, we attend a church service. The difference is way opposite from each other.

Modern church services are typically encased with a Broadway-type staged music performance. The sound played is so loud one cannot hear themselves sing out of key. At times it brings back memories of attending a rock concert. The teaching is also one-way communications. You might as well watch a video presentation of the talk. There is usually no exchange between speaker and listener.

When we gather together, one also wonders where people find their peaceful rest? With modern services so intense, we now find our peaceful rest during the remaining week. Maybe I'm only getting older and the only person who sees it that way. The majority probably have their act together better than I.

Meanwhile, imagine a life where your work is your worship to God. Where your motive and intentions are to glorify God. What level of quality would you display in your work for God's glory? How would you relate with your fellow employees if your work was to glorify God? How would you tackle that difficult customer if your work was to support God? If you own a business, does your brand, service, product, and culture emulate God's glory? If your work is your worship to God, how does that show up in your business?

Tough questions. But the fruit of worship yields unceasing motivation. When you discover Christ in everyday work, the activity becomes more meaningful. When your business reveals Him and his Kingdom, than your actions become your worship. To worship God through all you do makes life's journey more rewarding. Seize it. Ride it. Enjoy the life we have in Christ as we worship Him and serve others through the work we do every day.

Let your work worship our Triune God.

#301 – Free at Last

"They promise them freedom, but they themselves are slaves of corruption. For whatever overcomes a person, to that he is enslaved." 2 Peter 2:19

I am a reformed chocoholic. There was a time when I would eat pounds of chocolate each day. The food comforted me through the stress of everyday life. This went on for many years. Then one day at a grocery checkout counter I was shocked in my inability to say no in the acquisition of a chocolate bar. The reality sunk in that I was addicted to chocolate. I was a slave to my yearnings and desire for chocolate. I couldn't say no. I had lost my freedom of choice. Instead of choosing whether I wanted chocolate, the choice was already made. I was a slave to my desire for comfort and the satisfaction that chocolate gave me. The price I paid was my freedom.

Many of you may laugh, but for a highly disciplined person (I thought) this was serious. I was enslaved to something else rather than to Christ. The problem wasn't the chocolate. I was using physical means to please some inner spiritual hole. For me, that hole was the inability to cope with the everyday stress of work and life. Chocolate, with its built-in nutritional values seem to please that inner me. Yet was there something deeper?

Chocolate was the byproduct triggered by the challenges of work. What had to change for me to forgo my chocolate addiction? Jesus spoke about worry and stress as recorded in Scripture (Matt. 6:24-34). The bottom-line is having a stronger relationship with Jesus Christ at work. When I repented of my lack of faithfulness on the job, things began to change. I quit chocolate and discovered Spirit fruit. I learn to worry less and lean more on Him.

The more God's Spirit empowers us, the less physical things are needed to be satisfied in this life. Today, I don't miss the chocolate. I stay away from it because I would rather depend on Jesus. The more we lean on Christ and His finished work, the less enslaved we become to sin and outside cravings. The more He lives in us, the more freedom we have to live a fully, expressive life. Now whenever anything comes between Him and me, it is quickly thrown away. For we now know that real freedom is experienced when we surrender our inner being to the King.

#302 - Twenty Minutes, Twenty Days, Twenty Years

"What is your life? For you are a mist that appears for a little time and then vanishes." James 4:14

One of our small group member's Mom passed away this week. This past year along, his father and sister likewise died. The loss of three of your family members in one year is more grief than most of us sustain in any year. Yet, for us still alive and dealing with the challenges of life, death is sobering. Times like this allows us to pause for the moment to reflect on what is most important in our world.

This is when I most often think of the 20/20/20 concept. If you knew you only had twenty more minutes to live, what would you do? If you knew you only had twenty more days to live, what would you do? And what if you knew you only had twenty more years left to live, what would you do? At least once a year I ask myself these questions to be sure we are intentionally redeeming the time in our life.

By asking the twenty-minute question, I focus on those people who are most important in my life. I want them know I love them, appreciate them, and am rooting for them. I don't like to say good-byes. Instead, I let them know good tidings until we meet again.

The twenty-day question helps me focus on those important items that need to be completed. If I had only twenty more days left on this planet, would I be doing this? If it is important for someone in my world that I care about, I would still do it. Then there are those items that I always wanted to do but

117

always postponed them with the lazy excuse. If it is not important, admit it. If it is important, do it.

Then there is the twenty-year question. If you knew you had twenty more years to do something in this life, what would you do? This question helps you focus on your career or mission in life. Instead of trying to do everything overnight, you could easily start today. Then slowly work towards your personal worthwhile goal. As long as you are realizing your goal, you are being successful in your pursuit.

Your long-term goals add flavor to life. They allow you to fully express your talents. They give you meaning and purpose for your life. As you add value in other people's life, you grow from the experience. Your goals help you keep focused on the important aspects of life.

You can still take on other temporary projects. You may at times deviate from you plan. But you always return. One day you will look back and appreciate all God allowed you to experience. From the people to the events, your life was being enriched while HE prepares you for eternity.

So why not take the time today and ask yourself: twenty minutes? twenty days? twenty years? Your life is more than a bucket list. But your list keeps you focused on doing the most important aspects of life. When you look in the rear view mirror, you will have a better perspective of how God engineered events. The dots and people in your world will reinforce your faith in a living God's love for you.

#303 - Rules, Principles, or Character

"...by which he has granted to us his precious and very great promises, so that through them you may become partakers of the divine nature, having escaped from the corruption that is in the world because of sinful desire. For this very reason, make every effort to supplement your faith with virtue, and virtue with knowledge, and knowledge with self-control, and self-control with steadfastness, and steadfastness with godliness..." 2 Peter 1:4-6

After you acknowledge Jesus is Lord, what comes next?

The Bible outlines our journey into three phases: justification, sanctification, and glorification. Justification is about Christ's gift to humanity restoring our relationship with God. Glorification is the resurrection package. This is when our physical body is morph into a glorious state like our Lord's. Sanctification is the time between. This is where we grow in the grace and knowledge of Jesus Christ in preparation for eternity. This life-long period also gives us a mini-foretaste of Kingdom reality while on earth.

Sanctification is the now time. Most disciples of his start this journey first focusing on "the rules found in the Bible." The problem though soon hits them that life is not black and white. External, fixed rules are like the ABCs of grammar. You need to know them before you can start communicating with others. But they don't take you very far.

Then after becoming frustrated with rules, you realize you need greater flexibility. So, you begin to exert more emphasis on living with principles. Yet, over time you learn that principles are like words. Words better express what you want communicated than just knowing the ABCs. Yet words only expressed a tiny part of what you want known. We also need to form words into meaningful sentences. But then you realize there is more.

Enter character development. When you combine sentences, you make paragraphs. When you add paragraphs together, you get chapters. From chapters building upon each other, you complete a book. You have endured the process of knowing the basic ABCs to creating a work of art. Along the way you added personality and experiences. A similar exercise goes into building Godly character.

When you allow God's Spirit to enter you and lead you, you begin the process of character development. You begin to set aside the rules and principles for a transformed life of virtue. Virtue is holiness in action. It doesn't come overnight. It requires walking with our heavenly Triune God in all matters of life. It is the Spirit writing his love into our heart. He leads us to express mercy and justice from God's point of reference. It is more than head knowledge. It is eternal wisdom and understanding with Godly attributes placed into action. The result is a life that flourishes for all.

So the next time to think life is black and white with rules and principles, think again. Instead, ask the Triune God what would He have you do at a moment like this? You may be pleasantly surprised.

#304 - Let Love Lead in the Marketplace

"For when I am weak, then I am strong." 2 Corinthians 12:1

For many years, I thought sin was my biggest problem. Then one day a revelation occurred. Sin is not the main problem; a lack of love is. Yes, sin needs to be eliminated. But when our focus is on dealing with our weaknesses, our strengths become buried. In Christ, my sins are totally covered in grace. What I lack is the consistent hunger to allow Love's entrance into my heart and have its way with me toward others. When I am weak (the result of my sins or the sins of others impacting me) is when Christ becomes more alive in me.

When I look around the world and note the conflicts that are happening, where is the love? I see the sin, but where is the love? When I look at businesses and the conflict between employee and employer, where is the love? When marriages of thirty and forty years fall apart, what happen to the love?

It is easier to cover up the sins in one's life than always express one's attitude and action in love. If we invested more time praying and seeking ways to better love each other, sin would dissipate. We would spend less time sinning and more time strengthening our relationships.

Yes that includes the marketplace which cries out each day for love and compassion. The challenge is today's H.R. regulations frown upon physical hugs. So, we need to get creative and show others that we care and appreciate them.

There are many other ways to lead with love. I'm sure if you set your heart in making it happen, the Holy Spirit will open the doors to make it possible. Also, if you are hungry to share God's love with others in a business context, you are going to need his help. No matter how successful we become, we soon realize how poor we are of God's Spirit. We need more of God's Love to come in us and through us. We run empty at times for the amount of God's love we need simply to survive.

Yes, it may be radical to lead with love, but it is also the Kingdom way. It works.

#305 - Who Are You?

"...you are sons, God has sent the Spirit of his Son into our hearts, crying, 'Abba! Father!' So you are no longer a slave, but a son, and if a son, then an heir through God." Galatians 4:6-7

Whenever we meet someone new, the conversation reaches the question, "what do you do?" The reply is the job we have or the number #1 responsibility currently in our life. Like being a full time mom or a volunteer for a nonprofit. From this reply we quickly summarize a person's identity. This leads to whether we have something in common to discuss. Yet what we do and who we are may not fit into the standard cultural box of the time. That sometimes leads to an awkward conversation with the new person in our world.

One of the challenges many people face is separating the roles in their life from their identity. We see this with people who identify themselves through their roles. If they have a great day at work, they feel good about themselves. If they have a bad day at work, they feel less worthy. If the current fad is to be a celebrity or entrepreneur , they will pursue it as the answer for their life. The struggle is realizing the roles we choose may fill our identity cup but will never sustain it.

One of life's big questions is to answer "who am I?" What are my strengths, weaknesses? What is my purpose in life? Where do I fit in this world? The answer, as you may already be aware, is Jesus Christ. He is life's reason. He is the central character of the Bible. All life is built around Him. When we come to that realization, than and only then, will we discover our identity.

We will realize that He is the beginning of a new creation; a creation that includes you. You have an identity that is engraved in heaven and in your heart through the Holy Spirit. No role can match it. Nothing in this world will complete you and fulfill you like He will.

Whatever role you may pursue is something you do, not who you are. In your role you can learn new skills and improve your performance. Who you are is not measured by performance, but by the grace of God. Who you be is expressed by who you follow and serve.

Performance may measure outcome, but grace identifies the heart. Both are needed to survive in today's world. Yet, who you be will always survive your roles. Your role will come to an end. Yes, the role of husband, wife, father, mother will come to an end. Your function as an executive, teacher, scientist, or musician will come to an end. Being an athlete, actor, or whatever, will come to an end.

But, who you are and be, will continue into eternity. God is more concern of who you are than the role you perform. His purpose is to prepare you for eternity. He is not requiring you to climb the corporate ladder. Nor win the super bowl. Nor marry your childhood sweetheart. Those are roles He allows you to choose.

Let's not confuse our roles in life with our identity. It only leads to more frustration and heartache. Yet, when you accept and live life in Christ nothing will take away your identity. You are already included in the work Christ has accomplished. So, enjoy your life in Christ and be thankful for the various roles you are able to perform for HIS glory.

Remember, you are especially created for HIM. HE will lead you and prepare you for eternity. The role details are for you to choose. So don't confuse the two in determining who you are.

#306 - Jesus is King

"They will make war on the Lamb, and the Lamb will conquer them, for he is Lord of lords and King of kings, and those with him are called and chosen and faithful." Revelations 17:14.

The theme of the first four books of the New Testament, Matthew, Mark, Luke, and John, is about Jesus and the Kingdom of God. The four gospel accounts emphasize Jesus' triumphant victory over Satan, sin, and death. The story is about God becoming man. The God-Man teaching Kingdom principles. Plus Him fulfilling His purpose to be crowned King of Heaven and Earth.

We read the angel Gabriel's visitation to Mary (Luke 1:32-33) announcing she was to give birth to a King. Likewise the shepherds (Luke 2:11) and Magi (Matt. 2:2) saw and worshiped the Messiah. Jesus' birth, life, and death highlights his office as King, Messiah, and Lord.

Throughout the New testament we are also reminded Jesus is Lord of lords and King of kings. He is King over all the earth and heaven.

I write this as a reminder. Jesus gave a parable about the King coming and then leaving stewards to run his operation. (Luke 19:11). We need to realize the same.

The Kingdom of God is operating in today's world. It is being managed by stewards appointed through the Holy Spirit. Those who recognize Jesus as the King of the earth live under His domain. We witness this in small pockets within business, government, education, and families. His Kingdom is actively alive through his universal Church.

Yes, there is conflict between His Kingdom and the governments of this world. We have dual citizenship between heaven and earth. Many of us learn to take advantage of both domains. As subjects to the King, we have the freedom to choose who we serve first. Either we continue to prioritize service to our heavenly King, or rebel and sell our soul to the dark side. Whenever the world's government conforms to our Lord's Kingdom, we gladly serve. If the government rebels against our King's mandates, then we choose to support our King.

Many of us in this county don't understand the authority of a King. We place our individual rights based on law. But, when one realizes a King is the law, then one learns about healthy fear. Gratefully, we serve a proven King who has a heart that balances justice with mercy.

I am thankful to serve Jesus Christ as my King. How about you?

#307 - Living Dangerously with Integrity

"Better is a poor man who walks in his integrity than a rich man who is crooked in his ways."
Proverbs 28:6

In business, the temptation to earn a buck sometimes blinds us to the Godly action required at the moment.

I remember one businessman who admitted to having a poor long-term memory. He had difficulty remembering events and situations after several days. His remedy? He always spoke the truth and dealt honestly with every decision he had to make. His reason? If he needed to recall what he did in any situation, he would only ask himself "what was the right thing to do?" And that would lead him to what he did. He learned to live with integrity in all his business dealings and slept very good at night. And yes, he was very successful in his business.

There was another business man who reached the point he could start growing his market share. But he had difficulty developing an advertising program to properly brand his operation. Most of the recommendations given to him was based on image rather than what his core business was all about. Then one person asked him what was his primary core value. What did he want to emphasize with all his customers and employees. The answer: integrity. Thereafter, the successful idea led him to tripling his business. Wherever you looked, his brand was about integrity. And he lived up to his word. He guaranteed his service. He would refund money without question. He would keep his word even if it hurts. He walk the talk.

The enemy of integrity is pragmatism. Pragmatism is the philosophy that whatever works is good at the end. It is situational ethics without a standard. It focuses on outcome rather than the process. It generally produces short-term favorable results. But the long term ramifications are most often very unfavorable.

If you are a person of integrity, let your customers, employees, and vendors know. Not with words, but through actions. In today's marketplace, integrity is a marketing niche that many people gravitate towards. In fact, people who champion integrity, attract other like-minded people. Those without integrity will try to take advantage of you at first. And it may cost you a few dollars in the process. But after you refrain from doing business with them, they will change their way. For money has a way of changing a person's behavior. It may not be the Kingdom of God for them yet, but at least they can see it in action.

Imagine what a room full of motivated people with integrity could do? Wouldn't it be fun to operate a business and find out? Some may call that dangerous living. I call it being radical in Christ.

#308 – Christian

"...And in Antioch the disciples were first called Christians." Acts 11:26

The first time the word Christian is mentioned in the Bible is in Acts 11:26. The Greek word is Christianous. It basically means a follower of Christ. C.S. Lewis though like to refer it as "little Christs."

So when someone calls you a Christian today, are they comparing you to a smaller version of Jesus Christ? Or a religious fuddy-duddy?

In the first century, the title "Christian" was a derogative statement. A pun that translated to something like "follower of goody-goody. The disciples though took the title and transformed it into a positive statement. Thereafter Christian became known as a follower of Jesus Christ. Today we may call that redeeming an idea for Christ's Kingdom.

For are we not all ambassadors of Christ's Kingdom (2 Corinthians 5:20)? Do we not represent His ways with everyone we meet as a little Christ? Are we not a little Christ in the home with our family? Our associates at work? At the gym? The tennis court? While driving? Or eating at a restaurant?

The fact is we can't live like a little Christ doing it all ourselves. I know, many of us have tried. But what happens when we allow the Holy Spirit to live and transform our life from the inside-out? Doesn't our attitude and behavior begins to model King Jesus. Often, it even amazes us. For we know what this old man was like and is like. What we long for though, is the final development of the new creation. Until then, we only gather a few glimpses of what the new man will one day represent: a little Christ.

So do you want more, blessed excitement in your life? How about leaning on Him every day, everywhere, with everyone, as a little Christ? Then when someone points at you and calls you Christian, it will mean what God's intention is for all. A true representative of Him.

#309 - Lean On Him (LOH)

"Upon you I have leaned from before my birth; you are he who took me from my mother's womb. My praise is continually of you." Psalm 71:6

When you find out you are no longer the smartest, strongest, fastest, or whatever you are good at, what do you do? Maybe it is time to start, LOH.

When you realize you can't do it alone, others have failed you, and you don't know where to turn too, LOH.

When you finally admit you are broken and need help, LOH.

When your dreams are shattered, your hope disappears, or you feel forsaken, LOH.

When you come to the end of yourself, and can't go any further, LOH.

Or instead of waiting until you reach that moment of truth, you get ahead and start today. You may be surprised of the outcome when you first learn to Lean On Him.

Our Triune God wants you to have a life like His. Though we are limited by physical boundaries, He has wired us as a mini reflection of Himself. He wants you to learn and grow into His image. It all begins when you learn to lean on Him. How radical is that?

#310 - Truth. Reality. God.

"The Lord, who stretches out the heavens, who lays the foundation of the earth, and who forms the human spirit within a person..." Zechariah 12:1

In my sophomore year of college, I registered for a class in Ethics. But was denied because not enough students selected it as an elective course. Out of a 35,000-student body only 4 signed up for the class; not enough to justify paying for a teacher. In its place though, I took another philosophical course - Logic.

There we had enough students which allowed the administration to hire a teacher. The course trained us under the known arts of reasoning, decision-making, and truth-finding. But again, there were less than one dozen students in the class.

I didn't realize the ramifications of the event until some thirty years later. As we live this post-modern culture, we witness every day the distortion of basic logic. Today truth is relative. Decision-making is grounded on feelings. Reasoning is sabotage with lies, opinions, and prejudices. How is one to journey through life surrounded by this maze of noise and illusions?

When the foundation of a society is without a compass, any direction will do. If someone is able to identify North, then their search for home becomes easier. But without a North directional bias, every direction looks as good as the next. From my early camping days, we would classify that as being lost.

If one is serious to discover the truth of a matter, one needs to have a good grasp of reality. You find Reality among the foundational order of nature. Also the universal laws that govern existence. Order needs an order/law giver. In religious circles, this Law Giver is given the title God.

As one develops a relationship with God, one discovers His heart, mind, and character. From this and through various circumstances and situations, one comes to know HIM. Likewise you become known by the Creator of Life. Of all the gods known by 21st century standards, only one makes logical sense. Yet HE is the most misunderstood. The Bible reveals HIM as the Triune God: Father, Son, and Spirit. C. S. Lewis knew him. He converted from atheism to Christianity because Jesus Christ made the most logical sense. He compared the logic to the sun rising each morning.

So, if truth is important to you, then get the knowledge. Seek out the eternal facts, historical lessons, and scientific outcomes. Study the Creator of Life. Then you will have a stronger foundation to help you withstand the corruption around you.

#311 - Is Money The Answer?

"Bread is made for laughter, and wine gladdens life, and money answers everything." Ecclesiastes
10:19

The first pages of the Bible that I ever read was the Book of Ecclesiastes. As a seventeen year old seeker of God, I was stumped to understand the contents of the Book. What is so spiritual about physical pleasures? marriage? work? Is all vanity, blowing after smoke?

Yet the first scripture that I found excited as a young entrepreneur was the above. Living in a physical world requires physical necessities. Food, drink, and energy are some of the items we need to function. The above Scripture makes more sense than dollars (excuse the pun). In fact, 40 years later the Scripture has more meaning now than ever before.

For example, bread and wine are the dinner staples of Biblical times. Every dinner included the two. Jesus himself at the last supper took these two staples. And HE transformed them into an everyday memorial. Whenever we take bread and wine, we are reminded of Jesus. We commemorate his death, resurrection, and future return. (Maybe this is where the custom of saying prayer before each meal came from?).

Also, isn't bread shared between friends. It is a custom even as of today to invite people over for meals as a show of friendship and hospitality. Most often, bread is usually a staple of a meal surrounded by laughter and good conversation. Likewise, a little alcoholic wine loosens the heart and helps ease the emotional pain. Been so since the beginning of time. A little wine loosens the tongue and makes one feel a little happier. (Too much wine though causes one to lose control of their emotions and mental faculties). Yet in Biblical times wine was the main drink at weddings, festivals, and dinner. Jesus' first known miracle was changing water into wine.

Most people don't have a problem understanding bread is made for laughter. A few less with wine gladdens the heart. But money a solution to one's problems? Yet money is the answer for most of the challenges people face each day. With money, one is able to buy happiness (not joy) and freedom. Those without money lose out on opportunities. Ask yourself? How would the challenges you face each day be different if you had more money to throw at the problem?

In fact Jesus spoke about money more than many other topics. He didn't avoid the issue. Instead, he met it head on. His concern is when we make it a priority rather than secondary in our life. Yet money makes this physical world go around. If given the choice, how many would rather be poor than rich? Few I'm sure.

In this physical world, it takes money to operate. People need money to buy the necessities of life. Governments need money to operate. Even churches need money to cover the cost of ministries. Money answers many of the problems that confront them.

Again, the problem is when money becomes life's priority. But when your foundation is Jesus Christ, you keep your priorities in order. When you are in Christ, than the above scripture makes perfect sense. What do you think?

#312 - Where is Church?

"So the churches were strengthened in the faith, and they increased in numbers daily." Acts 16:5

In the New Testament the Greek word "ecclesia" is defined as an "assembly." The Greek word is most often translated "church" in the English language. Thus the word Church as signified in the Bible is an assembly of people. Today faith communities that meet in buildings identify themselves as a church. This is most often how most of us learn and identify a church. Yet is not a church larger than this?

One of the most eye opening revelations I have experienced pertains to the Church. The fact is the Church extends beyond the four walls of a faith community. Jesus made the comment that when two or three are gathered together in prayer, he is among them (Matt. 18:20). He didn't limit meeting together in a specific location. In fact, in John 4:21-23 HE stated that location wasn't important. But worshiping God in Spirit and Truth is the priority. So can't we say that where two or more believers come together in Spirit and Truth that Church is in session?

Wouldn't this mean that the Church is actively operating 24/7 non-stop around the globe? Is it not in session where two or more believers come together? Is it not in session where a husband and wife come together? Is it not in session where two believing employees of the same company come together? Is it not in session when two faith-driven neighbors meet together? Couldn't church take place when two or more come together at a golfing tournament? ballgame? party? grocery store? school? the beach?

What makes a Church? Is it the corporate legal structure? An organizational team? Or two or more coming together to share their faith, buildup one another, and glorify God in the process?

So what happens when one realizes Church is an assembly of people who trust and worship Jesus Christ? Doesn't that open the door for a 24/7 church service? As a believer, don't we walk in the presence of God all day and night? So when we sit through a one hour church service isn't that a continual process of doing church for the entire day? week? month? life?

Think about it.

#313 – Work

"But Jesus answered them, 'My Father is working until now, and I am working.'" John 5:17

Why work? Is it because we have too or because we want too? Don't people work for various reasons? For example:

Most people work for an income to cover their living expenses.

Yet some people work to express their God-given gifts.

Others work to enjoy the social interrelationships.

Some work to escape from internal problems.

Than some work because they have been asked to serve others in a specific capacity.

Others work to fulfill their obligations.

Many work to please some deep, driven-need.

Some work to earn a little extra income to help others.

Others work for a cause they believe in.

A few even work for the glory of God.

This is only a few of the reasons studies have shown why we work. Yet, the result of good work is the reason we have food, clothes, shelter, and transportation for the masses. It is the reason we have schools, hospitals, churches, and factories. It is the fruit of labor for the common good of all.

How about you? Is work a spiritual discipline that allows you to move with God in the arena of life? Or is work some kind of drudgery that is required while you serve your prison time on earth?

Jesus' stated that His Father God is working even as he spoke. That God didn't complete the creation of the world and then retired into His heavenly

138

home. Likewise, Jesus was purposely working instead of enjoying life on easy street. Jesus came to serve; and service requires work.

Work became difficult when Adam left the garden of Eden. That was the price for rebelling against Almighty God. God allowed mankind to taste what life is like apart from Him. But events have now shifted. Since the arrival of the incarnated Jesus Christ, man is now reconciled with God.

Work is now the means of grace that allows us to experience the fruit of God Himself. Even today, God is still at work.

We can now partner with Him in His work that includes the redemption of all creation. Believe it or not, that includes the work you do today. Ask yourself, how many ways can you glorify God today through your work? What if you took one way today and worship Him through your work. How radical would that be?

#314 - Follow The Money

"For where your treasure is, there will your heart be also." Luke 12:34

Want to know what your heart values? Just follow the money. Whether we are speaking about a business or a personal life, the principle is still the same. You can determine what you consider important by how you spend your money.

Take the example of a business that boasts their people are their most important asset. If you want confirmation, look at how they spend their operating expenses. What percentage relates to people?

You can do the same for a family. After the basic necessity of food, clothing, and shelter, where does the money go? This will give you a good snapshot of a person's heart; what they value and consider important.

Jesus' statement is still revealing today. What you value is where you will spend your time and money. Yet always remember. When the Triune God is the center of your soul, He is also redeeming your time and money. It is a process. But over one's life-time one learns that God owns it all. HE is simply sharing HIS wealth with us all.

That as stewards, we are accountable to Him. Thus, we thank Him for everything. This includes the opportunity to express ourselves through the physical activities of life. Like Him, we open our resources for others. Our values begin to change as the Holy Spirit changes our hearts to reflect Him more and more. We become more Christ-like.

We all express ourselves from our inner being. It takes a spiritual rebirth to have one's heart reshaped and molded into the image of the living God. When that happens, one then can say what the Bible states about King David. "He is a man after my (God's) own heart."

So if you are seeking a new adventure for life, ask God to reveal the condition of your heart. But more so, ask Him to change your heart to reflect His in everything you say, think, and do. Remember, He is rooting for you!

#315 - Growth Involves Discomfort

"...strengthening the souls of the disciples, encouraging them to continue in the faith, and saying that through many tribulations we must enter the kingdom of God." Acts 14:22

"Praise be to the God and Father of our Lord Jesus Christ, the Father of compassion and the God of all comfort" 2 Corinthians 1:3

Ever notice how much effort we spend as a society seeking comfort in all that we do? We buy comfortable clothes. We drive comfortable cars. We eat comfort food. We sleep on comfortable beds. We associate with friends who are comfortable. We parade through the day following our comfortable routine. We sit on our comfortable lazy chair. Yes, we even eat comfortable ice cream.

What happens when our comfortable lifestyle is disrupted? Don't we become upset and even traumatized? Have you ever notice how life has a way to interrupt our status quo? You begin to ponder if life is designed to force us into situations that need us to expand our comfort zone? So is it better to intentionally choose our discomfort? Or would you rather have "meteors from outer space" force you to change your routine? Isn't it when we exert energy toward a favorable outcome outside our comfort zone we actual grow from it?

When you complete a difficult assignment and receive a large bonus, are you not satisfied? When you start a new project outside your natural skills, is it not challenging at first? But over time, you master it and grow from it. It may have been uncomfortable at first, but afterward you grew by integrating the old into the new. Have you noticed that anything worth pursuing starts off at the uncomfortable level?

Paul wrote that entrance into the Kingdom of God is going to introduce tribulation. To move from comfort to discomfort is a prerequisite for entrance into God's Kingdom. To grow into the likeness of Jesus Christ is naturally discomforting. Get used to it! Quit your complaining. Get on your knees and cry out to God. It is the way faith in God is built. It is the way we grow in the faith. It is the way God help us to grow.

So when you find yourself discomforted, thank God. Roll up your sleeves, strengthen your praying arms, and cry out to God. It is the most successful way. It has been done since the dawn of life. Remember, you are privileged too share life with the Holy Spirit. You are involved in one of the God's greatest projects. He is birthing of a new creation. A new adventure awaits you. Besides, how else are we going to learn that He is our Comforter?

#316 - The Ultra-Lean Years

"For everything there is a season, and a time for every matter under heaven" Ecclesiastes 3:1

Ever notice that there is a purpose for every season of one's life?

Joseph was sold into slavery, imprisoned, and forgotten for thirteen years. Then through a series of "consequences" he became the governor of Egypt. The second in command to the Pharaoh.

David was anointed King of Israel at seventeen and wasn't crowned until thirty. For thirteen years he lived in the fields with a bounty on his head from the current king. His companions were the undesirables of his day. Yet he was being prepared to lead a country as he followed God.

Moses was raised as a prince in the Egyptian household. Fleeing for his life at forty for murdering a fellow Hebrew, he took up the occupation of a shepherd. The lowest of jobs in his time. For forty years he worked in the desert countryside. There the Lord prepared him at the age of eighty to lead his people back to their own country.

Each person had a call in their life from God, but the preparation time were the dry years. We would classify them today as the ultra-lean years.

Throughout history people used the lean years to prepare for the next season of life. During these years, one learns to cry-out and trust their Maker. One also learns humility and living graciously in preparation for greater service. Sometimes greater service may never come. But one is being prepared for more opportunities if they appear.

In business, the lean years allows one to focus on self-improvement. CEO's streamline operations, upgrade systems, and enhance the customer experience.

Whatever can be done with little monetary costs. For those businesses that survive, they come out stronger. They are more committed in serving their customers and stakeholders. If they didn't survive, then maybe it was time to try something else. One never knows what good is going to come out of a bad situation until it is written in history many years down the road. Until then, we learn to trust our Lord and walk with Him with our business and personal challenges.

In my own case, the best of times and the worst of times was in-between companies. It is during this time the cash flow dwindles, but the walk with God intensifies. When the doors of opportunity did open again, I always found my trust in Christ becoming stronger. And yes I was prepared to serve more effectively for another employer with God's gifts and love.

So remember, when you find yourself thinking you are forgotten by God, lean heavier. He is always there. He is only preparing you for the next season of life.

#317 - Undesirables of Jesus

"The Son of Man came eating and drinking, and you say, 'Here is a glutton and a drunkard, a friend of tax collectors and sinners.'" Luke 7:34

How many of us would condemn a person who spent their time partying with the low-life of humanity? (There is no low-life in God's eyes; but from mankind's perspective, there is).

You would of course need to define low-life. In Jesus' time, if you were not living the high-life, then you must have been considered the other. The high-life would be the people who had all the material aspects that life makes available. They would be seen high on the social ladder. They would be formally educated and successful in what they did. They would be recognized throughout the community. They may even be respected in the neighborhood. But, the low-life would be the undesirables of their day. In Jesus' time, that would include women, children, and the elderly. It would include slaves, the physically challenged, and the religiously inept. One doesn't grow up dreaming of becoming a low-life; life happens. The result generally is a life without great purpose, meaning, or self-sustenance. When people are broken and busted, they may become desperate. This may lead to stealing, prostitution, or homelessness. Most often they accept hand-outs for life's basic necessities.

Yet Jesus not only conversed with the undesirables of his time, He loved them. He enjoyed spending time with them and was even accused of being a "glutton and drunkard." His circle of friends included tax collectors, prostitutes, and the working class. His greatest supporters were women who provided for Him from their means. In Jesus' day, most women had no rights. They couldn't own property with minor exceptions. They were treated as collateral on the household books. Yet Jesus loved spending time with them.

He didn't spend time with them for a few moments as a political campaign video. He ate with them, drank with them, and conversed with them as a friend and teacher. He healed them. He fed them. He cared for them. He shared stories, laughter, and tears with them. He demonstrated the love of God, the service of God, and the heart of God with everyone He met. He treated others with respect and dignity. Wherever and whenever He could, he changed their world for the better.

How about you and me? Who are the undesirables in your world? What can you do today to impact the life of another that you wouldn't associate with in your daily walk? What if the next time you drove to work or went out for lunch, you took a closer look at the people you came into contact with. What if you ask God right then and there how you can take part with Him in the life of another. Just be ready for another adventure!

#318 – Good Work

"In the same way, let your light shine before others, so that they may see your good works and give glory to your Father who is in heaven." Matthew 5:16

What is good work?

We all can recognize it in our field of specialty. But to explain it to an "outsider" becomes another story.

In carpentry, it is where the corners and measurements are precise. Plus the look is picturesque.

In parenting, it is having grown children that are mature, responsible, and accountable. Both in the eyes of God and humanity.

In business, it is providing an economic service or product that benefits others. while maintaining a profitable operating model. Good work is recognized by one's peers.

But, does good work guarantee a productive outcome? The simple answer is no. You can develop the best "widget" on the planet, but if there is no demand for widgets, no one is going to buy the item. Even if there is a demand for the item, if no one is aware of your widget, no one again is going to buy the item.

Your peers may marvel at it. The product may be the best ever. It may represent the genius and character expressed through you. But no demand, no awareness, leads to no sales, and thus no profits. But good work!

Good work is only the reflection of the person or persons involved in the project. Good work is the outward expression of a person's inner character and mind. The person is presenting themselves through their actions. It is what each of us can control, change, and improve upon. The final outcome though involves others. It takes others to take part in sharing their good work that may lead to a more favorable outcome.

God wants us to follow His example and do good work. The outcome though involves more than our contribution. It involves others. God created the world which is a reflection of His good work. The outcome of its care though He has placed into the hands of others: humans. Isn't that the same thing we need to learn?

#319 – Who Jesus?

"Now when Jesus came into the district of Caesarea Philippi, he asked his disciples, 'Who do people say that the Son of Man is?'"
Matthew 16:13

When you want to gather information on a person's worldview, you can with a simple question. "What is your opinion of Jesus Christ?" Be ready though for anything. The person's reply may range anywhere from very friendly to strong animosity. You may have the best twenty minute discussion of the year. Either with a believer or non-believer than you would have every expected.

I like to throw the question out in the most unlikely places to see people's reaction. Some people are very comfortable to discuss their relationship with Jesus. Others keep their faith low keyed. But the conversations are always very revealing.

If they are agnostic or spiritually minded, it opens the door for further discussion. For I find that more and more people want to discuss questions about life. Why? Because most people shy away from the big three: religion, politics, and money. Yet each one is critical and important to discover one's purpose and freedom for living.

I am not being judgmental; nor am I seeking to evangelize. My goal is to seek-out a starting point of reference. From there, we begin a conversation that is personal and meaningful for the other person. In other words, we begin from their point of view rather than mine. And since everything begins and ends with God, why not start with Him?

Over the years, I have always been pleasantly surprised by some of the answers. Sometimes, I even found myself speechless. Which according to my wife is one of the most rare activities found under heaven. Yet, I have become more comfortable over the years to meet total strangers. And even extended family members to start off with the question: "Who Jesus?"

So the next time you find yourself bored and seeking some excitement in your life, why not. Why not become a little more daring and begin to ask others, "Who Jesus?" But be ready for anything.

#320 - Measureless Goals

"...the righteousness of God through faith in Jesus Christ for all who believe." Romans 3:22

In business, we measure all important outcomes. In fact, the old adage is if it is not being measured, then it isn't being managed. By measuring performance, feedback is gather to determine necessary improvements of outcome. Yet there are some objectives more difficult to measure than others.

Take for example one of life's undesirable outcomes: sin. The Bible defines sin in several different ways. John writes sin is lawlessness (I Jn. 3:4). James writes that "whoever knows the right thing to do and fails to do it, for him it is sin"(James 4:17). Paul also writes that whatever is not done in faith is sin (Romans 14:23). So how does one measure the outcome of faith?

Yes we could keep a journal log listing all behavior during the day. Then record next to each on a scale of 1 to 5 (5 is best) how faithful were we in that action. But would you give yourself a passing grade if you only scored a 2 out of 5? Would anything less than a 5 be labeled a sin?

Don't we typically measure sin by the outcome? If a person's behavior doesn't measure up to what "is Biblical" then we categorize it as sin. Yet Jesus came along and said that sin is even deeper than that; that sin is a matter of attitude and emotional heart. That we don't have to follow through with behavioral response. But just the inner thought of doing or not doing something can be classified as sin.

Am I being hard on managing sin? Or are we looking at the wrong side of the picture? Focusing on sin can become quite depressing. So instead of focusing on measuring sin, what if we focus on the opposite side? What if we focus on righteousness? Not our righteousness, but the Incarnate God's righteousness. What if we allowed more of His righteousness to abide in our life, would we even have to write about sin.

For is not sin the result of God's perfect love absent in us? Is not sin the absence of trust in our Triune God? Isn't lawlessness the absence of failing to yield to the King of Kings in our lives? Is not God's grace the answer to sin? Isn't His divine love, faithfulness, and influence immeasurable? Instead of trying to manage the sins in our world, what if we learn to better abide in the one who is measureless? Become more secure in His love, faith, and hope. Maybe there are some goals that don't need to be measured, but simply covered with God's grace. What do you think?

#321 - How Do We Draw Near To God?

"Draw near to God, and he will draw near to you." James 4:8

How does one draw near to God? For many of us, we walk the Christian journey with only a few tools in our soul-box. We focus on prayer, bible study, and fellowship. These are important. Yet most Christ-followers seem to stop there. They keep repeating the same three over and over again until it becomes so rote. That is when the joy disappears and routine duty takes over.

So do you want to have other tools that will reawaken the romance between you and our Lord?

A variety of *Disciplines* may be the spark that draws you nearer to Him. For those who are unfamiliar with disciplines, let me explain. They are the practices that help us focus our minds and bodies toward God. Mr. Richard Foster wrote a book entitled "The Celebrations of Disciplines." The book outlines practices by saints used throughout history to draw nearer to God. I would recommend the book for anyone who wants to add spice to their spiritual walk with the Lord.

These disciplines are the means of grace that allows us to imitate the mind and soul of God. The best discipline to choose is the one opposite of your natural disposition. For example, if you are very selfish with your possessions, you may want to practice the grace of giving. When you enable the Scripture "more blessed to give than to receive," you begin to destroy these chains. You begin to experience the joy that the Lord shares in blessing others.

If money controls you, you can practice the discipline of tithing. By giving away a percentage of your income to others, you again break chains binding you. You can give to your local church or a food pantry. The key is do it on a regular basis. As you do over time, the spirit of stewardship takes over.

Again, these acts by themselves will not cure you. It is the Spirit working within you. The Spirit will renew your heart and mind. As you practice these disciplines, you will draw closer to God. You will emulating Him more and more in everyday life. You begin to see life as He views life.

You also have to be careful that the discipline does not become more important than Jesus. We all have a tendency to find a discipline that drastically improves our walk with the Lord. We than falsely believe everyone else should practice the same thing in their life. We forget that we are all wired differently, yet the same. The disciplines that I need to practice to draw nearer to God may be different than yours. Yet our purpose is the same. We both want to walk closer with our Lord in our journey through life. Disciplines may help you in the process.

#322 - Lead People; Manage Systems

"...for if someone does not know how to manage his own household, how will he care for God's church?" 1 Tim. 3:5

One problem I noticed with new supervisors is the tenancy to manipulate people. In most cases, they do not realize what they are doing. They behave in a way to get the results they seek.

We also see this with parents rearing children. When one has young children, it is easy for the parent to control the actions of the child. They can use fear and punishment to produce the results they desire. But, as the child grows and becomes a teenager, the parent needs to adjust their leadership skills. For then, the child begins to reason and think for themselves. They are not afraid of the same consequences of their earlier childhood. Now the parent needs to take the time to reason and debate with the young adult. If not, the child will rebel, and the conflict becomes a war zone. Likewise, when the child becomes a full adult, the relationship again changes. The parent cannot use the same techniques from childhood with their adult child. Now the relationship is less about control and more about freedom of choice. The consequences may be the same, but the means change.

The same is true in the business organization were adults work with adults. Novice supervisors confuse the management of systems with the leadership of people. When one focuses on trying to manage people like systems, conflict will arise. Systems are designed to move through a process to do a specific goal. People however are led through engagement and expectations of consequences. Systems are logical, heartless, and predictable. People are emotional, soulful, and unpredictable. Systems can be quickly changed and modified for expected results with little feedback. People need time to grow and mature until full mastery of the workload is learned.

Don't confuse systems and people. Each are necessary for an organization to realize its potential. Yet both need a different approach. For example, God doesn't work with people the same way he works with animals. Animals are born with instinct. People are born with learned behavior. The animal's potential is limited. The person's potential is unlimited. Lead your people with the realization that their potential is greater than yours. But manage your systems with the realization the process makes your business unique. But don't confuse the two when working with each. Manage systems, but lead people.

#323 – Making All Things New (Christmas)

"And He who sits on the throne said, 'Behold, I am making all things new.'" Revelation 21:5

Christmas means so much more for me than a celebration of the birth of Jesus. The reason for the season is an annual reminder that God is still moving his story toward a happy ending! Today, the Son of God is now wrapped by human flesh sitting on his throne in heaven. HIS commission is to make all things new. Humanity is now witnessing the fulfillment of God's strategy. Jesus is expanding his Kingdom.

The birth of Jesus in human skin is God's universal plan to unite divinity with flesh. In Christ, we are reminded that all life is important. There is purpose and meaning behind every human being. Also that real sacrificial love is the answer.

The apostle Peter gave his first public sermon on the day of Pentecost. The same day the Holy Spirit made his public appearance. When HE did, Peter quoted from the prophet Joel:

'In the last days, God says, I will pour out my Spirit on <u>all</u> people. Your sons and daughters will prophesy, your young men will see visions, your old men will dream dreams.

As we look back these two thousand years, we witness the explosion of knowledge. We see sci-fi visions becoming reality. We have seen advancements in the human domain. Today, the nations are challenged not only to feed their people, but to provide avenues of education. To help them discover their purpose and potential in living a meaningful life.

We may disagree on methods, techniques, and strategy. But the God-centered life will continue to lay the foundation of common sense. God continues to place an extreme high value for life. HE also provides opportunities for you to discover life's meaning and purpose.

Jesus Christ is on his throne and He is making all things new. He has purchased all humanity through his life, death, and resurrection. He is the only person who has demonstrated real leadership for the benefit of mankind as a whole. His heart wants all to partner with him in his work now and into eternity. But he will not force you to comply. He respects your free will, and wants you to know he is always there for you. He is rooting for you, and wants what is best for you.

He is making all things new and wants you to know you are included with him in his plans. So, celebrate the season, rejoice with Him, and let love always be your leading guide.

#324 - Business is a Ministry

"Man shall not live by bread alone, but by every word that comes from the mouth of God."
Matthew 4:4

Does God only work within the four walls of a faith community?
There are days when I sit in a church service the preacher seems to indicate that is the case. That God's special blessing is only upon those who serve within their faith community.

Somehow, what I do from Monday through Saturday is spoken like a lower-level necessity. That the only real meaning to life lies between the four walls of the congregation. Now maybe it's me. But after all these years I long for ministers whose pastoral is larger than their micro faith world. Somehow it seems we forget that God is attuned to the world. That our faith community is only a microscope of a much larger picture.

Take service for example. I sometimes get tired listening to preachers emphasize church service over other types. It's like "church service" is the only service that is approved by God. Whatever else one does outside of the "church" doesn't compare. Again, maybe it is me, but the Bible doesn't delineate service into sacred and secular. Humans do. I have seen people who serve to please a personal ego within the faith community. Instead of having God's Spirit fill the void, they seek everyday carnal desires. Whether status, power, prestige, money, or fulfillment, they do it in the name of church service.

Within the religious world, we call it ministry. In the marketplace, we call it service. The goal is the same. To provide and care for the people who have needs that we can satisfy. But "ministry" makes it sound holy. "Customer Service" makes it sound self-serving. Yet have we not seen people within church ministry glorify themselves? And again, in the marketplace, haven't we seen the same? Yet within the church, haven't we also seen more often people who serve for the glory of God and for the sake of others? Then again, don't we also know people who serve in the marketplace for God's glory and for the sake of others?

Am I too bold to say that God also created business? That business is a ministry for the economic benefit of others? Jesus quoted that "man shall not live by bread alone, but by every word that proceeds from the mouth of God."

In the church world we emphasize God's Word. Outside of the church world, people emphasis the economic necessities. Is one more important than the other? Doesn't it take both, the Spirit of God and the physical necessities of life to live a full, meaningful life? Maybe it's time we stop segregating the world into us versus them. That we are more important than them. Maybe it is time we realize that the Triune God considers all labor and service important. That ministering the Word and the physical necessities are both important and necessary. That one without the other leaves a person poor, hungry, and blind.

Thus the next time you are asked to participate in someone's ministry because you don't seem to have one, let them know. You already are in a full time ministry. Your business is a ministry for God's glory and for the economic wellbeing of others. Or is that too radical for you?

#325 - Segmentation or Coherence?

"There is neither Jew nor Greek, there is neither slave nor free, there is no male and female, for you are all one in Christ Jesus."
Galatians 3:28

In the apostle's Paul's world, there was a Jewish prayer that thanked God for not being a gentile, slave, or female. Being in any one of these categories was frown upon by the Jewish religious leaders.

As was and still is the custom, humanity likes to categorize each other into certain groups. Usually our view is segregated by our status or position in life. It was no different in Paul's time. If one was Jewish, they were superior to the gentile. If one was a free person, they were superior to the slave. If one was a male, they were superior to a female. Yet Paul wrote to the Galatians that one is not superior to the other. That superiority lies in Christ and we are all on even ground in our relationship with Him.

So what does this mean to us in the twenty-first century?

If we are followers of Christ, then we know He died for the whole world. That mankind has been forgiven before even asking to be forgiven. That God has re-opened the door for mankind to have a direct relationship with Him. Theology defines this as justification.

What does this mean in practical terms?

No matter your nationality, station in life, or sexual orientation, Christ died for you. In dying, the God-Man redeemed the entire human race. That includes you, me, and every person who is alive, died, and yet to be born. He made us brothers and sisters one with Him and each other. He provides an even playing field for everyone.

Whether we serve in church or outside the four walls of our faith community, it doesn't matter. We are included in Christ. If you work in the nonprofit industry, education, or medical world, Christ includes you. If you are employed in government, or the business marketplace, you are included in Christ.

As representatives of His domain, we walk with Him. We work with Him to restore relationships, values, and structures. We are first His servants. Called to partner with Him in His work restoring creation to His original intent.

Segmentation is how this world's system categorizes people, ideas, and events. Christ came so that we could focus first on Him. He is the central core of life. He breaks down the walls that prevents us from loving each other. He trains us to bless each other and serve one another. No human is greater than the other. We have equal standings before the King.

As we walk in the Spirit, we are united with Him. We also unite with each other. We then come to the realization that universal coherence comes by living life in Christ. Or is this too radical for one to accept?

#326 - Kingdom of God in the Marketplace

"Being asked by the Pharisees when the kingdom of God would come, he answered them, 'The kingdom of God is not coming in ways that can be observed, nor will they say, Look, here it is! or There!' for behold, the kingdom of God is in the midst of you." Luke 17:20-21

Where is God's Kingdom in the Marketplace? For most of us we witness a taste of God's Kingdom within the faith community of our church. For others, the Kingdom of God is found within the four walls of home. Again, for others it may be the one morning each week Bible study. There you find the fellowship and sharing which sparks enthusiasm for the rest of the week. Yet where is God's Kingdom in the workplace?

The above scripture use to puzzle me. How could Jesus tell the unconverted Pharisees the Kingdom of God is within each of them? Is not the Kingdom of God the rule and reign of Christ? These Pharisees didn't believe Jesus was who He claimed to be. He wasn't their King. So how could they be under the authority of Christ?

There lied the problem. The Kingdom of God is the authoritative government of God ruled through the Spirit of God from the heart. It is the soul that submits to Christ's authority that is a willing subject. All souls are under the authority of Christ. Yet, the soul that rebels against Christ is walking down a dangerous path. The connecting point is a matter of the heart. The heart that mutually submits one to another in service of the King of Kings is a servant of the Kingdom. The heart that rebels against the King of Kings is a lost and confuse child of God. They are disallowing themselves a meaningful relationship with the Triune God.

164

Again, the Kingdom of God is in the marketplace through the hearts of believers who are subject to the King. Wherever two or three are gathered, Christ is among them hearing their prayers (Matt. 18:20). The Kingdom of God is not limited behind the four walls of a faith community. The Kingdom of God is active within every organization where two or three assemble in His name. In business, the marketplace, and wherever Christ-followers are serving, God's Kingdom is operating. How do we affirm this? Watch when people profess and subject themselves to the King of Kings. Look for the fruit of God operating between people. So how about your marketplace? Is it too radical to allow God's Kingdom an entrance into your workplace?

#327 - Jesus the Carpenter

"Is not this the carpenter, the son of Mary and brother of James and Joses and Judas and Simon?"
Mark 6:3

"And when Jesus was baptized, immediately he went up from the water, and behold, the heavens were opened to him, and he saw the Spirit of God descending like a dove and coming to rest on him; and behold, a voice from heaven said, 'This is my beloved Son, with whom I am well pleased.'" Matt. 3:16-17

What we know about Jesus comes mostly from the gospels. He entered into public ministry around the age of thirty (Luke 3:23). Before that time, he worked as a carpenter in the family business (Mark 6:3).

A carpenter during the first century was more general than today's specialist. Today, carpentry is classified in many categories. There is rough carpentry and finish carpentry. There are specialists in roof replacement and cabinet making. In Jesus' time, carpentry involved the whole gambit. Everything including general contracting, cement block building, and wood carving. Jesus, most likely, ran the family carpentry business after the death of Joseph. He was the eldest and Jewish tradition gave the senior role to the first born.

What makes Matthew's witness come alive at Jesus' baptism? The fact our Heavenly Father made this statement BEFORE Jesus' public ministry. The statement was that He was "well pleased with His Son." Again, the statement was made BEFORE his Messiah ministry. After watching Jesus conduct the routine matters of everyday life, HE praised HIM. Approximately thirty-years of personal , family, and business affairs, His Father was please.

Our Father loved Jesus not because of what He accomplished. Or did not do. Or was planning to do. But simply because He loved Him. Up-to-that-time, Jesus lived a private life. Before the fame, glamor, and public testimony, Father God was well pleased with Him. Before the miracles, healings, preaching, and teaching, Father God was pleased with Him. Before the Last Supper, trial, death and resurrection, Father God was pleased with Him.

Our Father God loves us so much more than we may ever recognize. Every sacrifice, every act of kindness, and every matter done for His glory is known by Him. What we do doesn't increase His love for us. It's not about the praise nor fanfare. It's not even about the outcomes. It is having a personal relationship with the God of the universe. He knows you because He designed you, gifted you, and prepared a place for you in His plan.

We now live in Christ. We look forward to the time when the same words from Matthew 25:21 are spoken to us: "Well done, good and faithful servant. You have been faithful over a little; I will set you over much. Enter into the joy of your master." Imagine what a difference a carpenter walking with the Triune God could do today? Whether in his business, family, or community? Or is this just too radical for someone to believe?

#328 - God's Plan For You

"For thus says the Lord: When seventy years are completed for Babylon, I will visit you, and I will fulfill to you my promise and bring you back to this place. For I know the plans I have for you, declares the Lord, plans for welfare and not for evil, to give you a future and a hope. Then you will call upon me and come and pray to me, and I will hear you. You will seek me and find me, when you seek me with all your heart. I will be found by you, declares the Lord, and I will restore your fortunes and gather you from all the nations and all the places where I have driven you, declares the Lord, and I will bring you back to the place from which I sent you into exile." Jeremiah 29:10-14

Whenever I hear a sermon encouraging God's people with the above Scripture, I cringe. Most of the time I hold my breath. Why? Because someone most often will use this Scripture out of context to illustrate a point. I have been taught to first read Scripture in context. Then understand its cultural and historical significance in its time. Afterward, then expound its application into today's culture. Most of the time this scripture is used as a short cut to motivate people to trust God with their future plans.

But when read in context, one quickly recognizes that the Lord made a specific promise to Israel. After being disciplined through seventy years of exile, He will restore their nation. A specific prophecy for a specific nation for a specific time in history. What this scripture reveals is the Lord's purpose will always be accomplished.

What does this mean for you and me?

- God has a plan He started at the foundation of the universe that includes you.

- It is God's plan, not yours or mine.

- Our plans most likely are not God's plan.

- The earlier we learn to accept God's plan, the quicker we will experience a relationship with Him.

- As we develop a deeper relationship with Him, the greater His Spirit lives in us. He begins to influences us, and empowers us to live life the way He originally created life too be.

- The brokenness of sin slowly dissipates from our lives. Righteousness becomes our garment. Sin is replaced with the riches of His eternal presence. - We don't have to wait for heaven; heaven arrives now in Christ as He lives in us.

We do not have to take scripture out of context to make a point. God has a plan that includes you and me. His desire is for all humanity to join him within the Triune God circle. Today, we are heirs, children, and servants of the King of Kings. He lovingly invites us now to take part in His work. So we gladly join HIM as HE redeems all creation into His original intent (Romans 8:20-21).

So why misuse scriptures to make a point? Is not the truth already good enough?

#329 - Jesus Wows Me Again

"O Lord, you are my God; I will exalt you; I will praise your name, for you have done wonderful things, plans formed of old, faithful and sure." Isaiah 25:1

It seems most of the time when I study the scriptures into the life of Jesus, another Instagram moment hits me. Have you ever notice Jesus' response when meeting someone who exercises faith in God? He affirms the moment with words of praise and encouragement!

Take for instance:

The Syrophoenician woman in Mark 7:24-30;

The centurion in Luke 7:1-10;

The prostitute in Luke 7:44-50;

The hemorrhaging woman in Luke 8:40-48.

In each of these moments He recognized the person's faith in Him. Not a blind faith in something out in the universe. He not only recognizes it, but uses it as a teaching moment. Like a sales meeting acknowledging someone's achievement for the week. He praises the act and the person's belief and trust in Him.

Whatever the situation, He would recognize God's influential impact at the moment. And then share the moment for the sake of others.

How about us? Do we acknowledge God's manifestation in our journey? Not just to ourselves but with people we meet and associate with each day. Why not take a moment and share your experience with others? What better way to share your faith with others? Consider this another way to be radical in Christ for God's glory and for the sake of others.

#330 - Blessed Test or Repeat

"The crucible is for silver, and the furnace is for gold, and the Lord tests hearts." Proverbs 17:3

How are you when it comes to tests? Does your palms sweat? Does your stomach turn into knots? In those undergraduate days, I hated tests. But I was blessed with an excellent short term memory. So I would cram the day before the exam, take the exam, and score a high grade. But don't ask me the same questions the following week. I wouldn't be able to recall. Yes, I studied for an exam grade; learning was on the lower rung of the priority ladder. Then in graduate school, the attitude changed. Exams were excited. Why? Because I loved the majority of classes and learning was a prime motivation. I didn't really care about the grade. The result was better grades and mastery of the subject material. Why does this matter?

The Bible states that we will be presented with life tests (Ps.11:5, Pr.17:3, I Thess. 2:4). A time when you will face a moment of truth. A time when the results will reveal the true character of your soul. These tests will not be multiple choice, essay, or mathematical formulas. They will typically confront us with two primary choices. The choice to live within the circle of the Triune God fellowship or outside the circle. In either circle God remains with you. The difference has to do with eternal rewards and the difficulty of your walk through life.

For example, Adam and Eve failed their test and forced to live outside the Garden of Eden. Abraham chose to obey. He was ready to sacrifice his one son. Yes God intervened at the last moment. Abraham was rewarded for passing his test of faithfulness(Gn. 26:5).

Jacob wrestled with the Lord (Gen. 32:24-26). He likewise passed God's test for persistence and endurance. Joseph was tested through slavery and prison. But he also remained faithful and obedient to God's integrity. Saul was made the first King of Israel but failed the test. He was disowned and replaced by David.

Jesus was led into the wilderness by the Holy Spirit to be tempted by Satan. (temptation is not a sin; temptation draws-out personal desires that could lead to sin). Jesus was tempted with immediate governmental, religious, and economic leadership (Lk.4:1-13). But HE trusted His Father will work out the plan at HIS time and didn't take things into his own hands. He was faithful to His Father's desires and passed the test.

In business, many opportunities will come to make large sums of money. The problem isn't making money. But the manipulation, deceitfulness, and witchcraft played out to win the "prize." Is this God testing you or blessing you? Or is this God blessing you and testing you? Like all moments of truth, you will not know until later in life.

Are you willing to sacrifice character, virtue, and integrity for the "golden fleece?" Our reward comes from being faithful to Life's Provider. The reward is to live and conduct business within the Triune God's circle. During the test, will you faithfully and honestly support God who knows you better than anyone? Will you wait, listen and hear his suggestion before committing?

The aim is twofold. To be honest with all parties through the entire process. Plus focus on glorifying God with the end result. When you remove God's purpose from the picture, you then cloud the process. Will you allow your selfish desire and behavior bring a failing test to the Master's feet? The outcome is a good reflection and snapshot of where your soul stands before God.

Again, life tests will come in the marketplace. The choice is usually between more Mammon or fulfilling your word with others and God. Your response will reveal where your heart is compared to God's mirror. You will either rejoice with God or continue to hang on the far edges with more refining to be done. But no matter the outcome, God's grace always is open for you to repent and learn from the situation. HE will never leave you nor forsake you. He is rooting for you.

Your choice is how diligent you want to cultivate your soul. So when you fall short, repent. Then start over again. God is merciful and knows our weak condition. Through the tests we discover where we actual stand in comparison with HIM. Our need for a savior becomes more real. So our heart leans more on HIM. He strengthens us in our ordeal. Over time, you will overcome and not need to repeat the matter. You character is being refined for His glory. He gets the credit. You gain the benefit. Or is that too radical for you to believe?

#331 - The Principle of Three

"This happened three times, and the thing was taken up at once to heaven." Acts 10:16

T he number three is an old friend. Over the years, I have seen whenever (s)he shows up, life becomes better. (S)he is my friend. I have seen over and over again how (s)he relates with others in similar favorable circumstances.

We have observed our old friend three from the beginning of creation. In Christ's life on earth. Plus in the far reaches of the marketplace. Three is a proven friend. (S)he continues to give greater assurance for one's choices, accomplishments, and relationships.

You first notice three in our Creator God: Father, Son, and Holy Spirit: One God in Three Persons. The Lord instructed Israel to gather together in a holy assembly three times a year (Deut. 16:16). When Job lost his entire health, family, and fortune, his three friends came to him (Job 2:11). Daniel was educated for three years and prayed three times a day (Dn:1:5,6:10). You notice Christ faced three temptations in the wilderness (Lk.4:4-12). Jesus was most intimate with three of his disciples (Mk. 5:7, 9:2, 14:33). When Peter denied Christ, he did it three times (Jn.13:38). When Christ extended his grace upon Peter, he ask Peter three times whether he loved Him. Jesus died and was resurrected after three days (Jn.21:15-19). Whenever two or three people are gather together, Christ is among them (Mt:18:20). The best is to have two or three witnesses (Mt:18:16) whenever someone is being accused. Even the new Jerusalem coming down from heaven shows each side of the city to have three gates (Rev 21:13).

Three became a closer friend when I traded the stock market. I learned technical trading by viewing three different time frames. In fact, many of my trading patterns are three bar setups.

In measuring work performance during the day, the number three is a productive friend. How does one focus on the important issues of the day while dealing with urgent emergencies all day long? By trusting your number three friend. In various leadership roles, I always focus on three important goals each day. All this while still juggling the daily routine and urgent matters of each day. It also contributed a sense of self-worth when it felt like nothing got done but the movement of paper. Plus it let me know when I could quit for the day - after our three objectives where done.

Even when seeking God's Will in life, we have learned to invite the old friend into the equation. We align God's Word. We wait for the Spirit's inspiration. Then gather facts from as many affected parties to determine the course of action. The Bible instructs us that a threefold cord isn't easily broken (Eccles:3:4).

So why not take time out this week and look up the number three in the Bible. View how often the number three appears in decisions, circumstances, and relationships. The number is not a magical genie; just another way to deal with life. Maybe Father-Son-Spirit imprint is more prevalent in our everyday created world than we realize. Or is that too radical to believe?

Yes, real freedom is found only in Jesus Christ; not in a religion, crusade, nor great cause. So if you haven't experienced real freedom yet, maybe it is time to do business with the Lord. Ask him, seek him, and knock on the door that He presents. He will lead you to experience His freedom. The freedom that comes through an intimate relationship with Himself. He has been doing it for almost 2,000 years with a long list of testimonials. So unless you don't want to be free, why not today? It is a great day to celebrate freedom.

#332 - Making Decisions

"Where there is no guidance, a people falls, but in an abundance of counselors there is safety."
Proverbs 11:14

Personal decisions have a greater impact into other people's lives than we realize. When Adam & Eve decided to take the forbidden fruit, did they consider all the consequences? In a recent decision you made last week, did you consider all the people who owned a part of the decision? Did you consider all the ramifications? Most likely no. The majority of us don't unless we are reminded.

What the story of Adam and Eve demonstrates is how our personal desires blind us from a better solution. The pull to immediately please our personal desires is a strong human tenancy. There is one effective technique I've learned over the years to combat such behavior. Before making any decision is to list at least three other parties who may be affected by the outcome. From that list, I contact each one for their opinion of the impact of the decision in their world. From their answers, we do our best to develop a solution that will be best for all parties. Some may benefit better than others, but all need to benefit in some way.

Imagine if Eve followed in such a manner. She would have taken the serpent's statements and asked herself who else is impacted by this potential decision. Her list of three would include Adam, God, and the serpent. If she had spoken beforehand with God, He would have given her the consequences of such an action. If she discussed it with Adam, he would have given his view of the situation. Likewise, even though the serpent is a deceiver, one could match his replies with God's and Adam's. The result is a better overview to determine the best course of action. Do you think if she followed such an approach that the world would be in a different place today?

This is a simple approach that has served well over the years for many leaders. The challenge is to always put in place the same process each time. Otherwise, the time one fails to follow through is the one event causing one's world to fall apart. Again this is another simple approach to manage the many decisions one makes. Or is this too radical for you?

#333 - The Joy of Business

"As each has received a gift, use it to serve one another, as good stewards of God's varied grace." 1 Peter 4:10

Every person and every organization operates from a built-in structure of values. These values are built around an internal belief system. Studies have shown many of the values are shaped within us by the time we reach the age of eight or nine. These same values remain with us until some event changes our perspective of life. Only then, we may consciously or unconsciously make the change.

In business, the founder usually sets the belief/value system of the organization. She or he sets the standards others learn to follow if they want to be accepted within the business circle. As an organization grows, others step up to influence their values into the operation. Over time team leaders learn to work with one another though they may disagree with the values of others.

As a Believer in the marketplace, God has allowed us to partner with Him as His hands and feet. We join Him to economically serve others in the process. Also in the process, He works out His plan of redemption. So as a servant in God's government, we have new standards that we are learning. Yet we also have old values that need unlearning. In summary, God is training his children within the marketplace. That is if we choose to take part with Him in the process.

Why is this critical to understand? Because many of us enter the marketplace with a focus only on monetary reward. We believe that the sole purpose of business is to make money. So we make business decisions solely for a financial return. We seek a return of investment. A monetary payback for our time and effort. Yet is that how God views business?

Without getting heavy into theology, let's explore. Did not God give mankind instructions to have dominion over the earth? To manage it and to sustain it? Where in the creation account did God say our economic primary purpose is to make a profit? Yet didn't Jesus himself quote scripture that man needs bread and the Word of God to sustain himself? So what is the purpose of business?

Is not business a ministry that God ordained to provide for our fellow man? Like every ministry, is not the purpose to glorify God while we serve others. Don't we exercise the talents and skills HE has blessed us with? Is it not a joy to conduct business where God is glorified. Where all stakeholders benefit. Where we receive an economic return so we can do it all over again?

As a young, shy man starting out in the business world, I went into the accounting field. Why? Because I was good with numbers, logic, and able to bring order out of chaos. I didn't want to work with people. Likewise, I chose the real estate industry. Again, why? Because one could work with buildings and tangible property rather than with people. A funny thing happened along the way. I discovered that accounting, real estate, and business is all about people. That if one wants to succeed in life, one needs to go outside their comfort zone and learn. In my case how to communicate, relate, influence, encourage, and lead people. I learned the importance of developing long-term relationships. The emphasis on giving others my best for their highest benefit. We became successful operating efficiently while adding value for our customers. The profit we earned was the byproduct. We considered it the cost of doing business. In the end, our profit margins was the result of the emphasis of the value and service we provided.

Imagine if every business selected a product or service that would glorify God? If they wholeheartedly and honestly served people? Plus made enough money to stay in business; and continue to do it over and over again. What a wonderful world it would be!

When one reaches this point, then one can see the fruit of one's service and product through the eyes of God. Most people would think that this is impossible in today's world. Yet, is anything impossible with God? The problem is most people run business their way. They rather not yield and trust a living God who wants to partner with you in His mission for the marketplace.

Did not Jesus say if we seek His Kingdom first, that all these other things will be added to us? Does not that also include our business ventures? Yes there is joy in business when one learns to trust and rest in the living God. Or is that too radical for you?

#334 - Oops: Too Far?

"But each person is tempted when he is lured and enticed by his own desire." James 1:14

Notice how some of us love to take things to the far edge? When driving the car, we speed along approximately 9.9 miles above the speed limit. Why? Because we know that is the limit police radars are set. Or, since we know three beers is our limit before we begin to get tipsy, we stop ourselves at 2 3/4 bottles. We watch movies with violence because we know it is all make believe. Yet we twitch in pain when the scenes are so graphic that our stomach turns somersaults. But do we ever ask ourselves how much violence is ok for the heart to absorb before it becomes numb?

My mother had a very low tolerance for risk in her children's lives. She didn't want us to get burn with our hand on the stove, so she would tell us not to get close to the stove. But how far is to close? four feet? two feet? six inches? The closer we came to the stove and nothing happened, guess what? The closer we came the next time. Until that one day when we realized it wasn't how close, but how close without touching it.

One day I came to realized mother's instructions weren't true. That one could get close to the stove without any harm. So I began to question her instructions of not touching it. If she lied about being harmed by getting to close to it, is she also lying about touching it? So there was only one way to find out. I touched it. Truth behold, nothing happened. Was everything my mother told me a lie? So everyday thereafter I started each day with the habit of touching the stove. I was invincible. No stove could hurt me. Then one day, I skipped through the kitchen and reached out to touch the top of the stove.

But this time what I didn't realize was the stove top was turned on. Of course, by this time I didn't merely touch the top of the stove with a finger or two. I would slap my entire hand on the circular outlines. I will spare everyone the emergency details, but it is safe to say I didn't intentional ever do that again.

Yet isn't that how we operate within our relationships? Within our business transactions and life's decisions? We know life is a bell shape curve with two extreme ends. One end discerns what is good behavior and the other what is not good behavior. It is the middle 80% that is gray and subject to personal interpretation. It is in the gray areas that we push the limits. Or do we accept the results in gratitude as a gift from God?

Studying God's Word though opens the door for us to gather wisdom from His perspective. His way is an eternal one. We generally view life like a four-year old that must stand on his toes and reach over his head to touch the top of a stove. We don't see what is up there, but must rely on someone we can trust. Most often we learn it is our misunderstanding that leads us into trouble.

When the serpent tempted Eve with doubting questions (Gn.3:1-6), she could have taken the issue to God. But instead of bringing both parties together to find the truth, she made a poor choice. Eve made a decision apart from having the total picture. She took it upon herself, having only half the story, to divorce God. In management we call that a poor process of determining the best outcome. In counseling, we call that poor communications. In the Book of Proverbs (18:17) it states that one side seems right until the matter is heard from the other side.

Could Eve have been hanging out more with the serpent than with the Lord or Adam? How far is too far before one slides over the edge within a relationship? How close did she travel by the tree on her daily walks? How far do we push the limits before we go over the edge? Where is the edge? Are we sure or guessing? What happens when we lose our balance near the edge? Do we have enough rope in place to pull us to safety? Tough questions that only you can determine the answer. We all have different levels of tolerance for risk in our life. My recommendation is always seek wise counsel. Preferably from all sides before pushing any boundaries.

Also always remember, when Jesus is the center of our world, it is rare that we say oops: too far. For He keeps us balanced between the edges. That is why the relationship is more important than the rules. Rules will fail us. But He did not, does not, and will not.

#335 - The Greatest Blessing

"By this we know that we abide in him and he in us, because he has given us of his Spirit." 1 John 4:13

During a recent small group breakfast conversation, this question arose. "What is the greatest blessing you can receive in this life?" The answered varied depending on each person's journey through life. Some answered "a large family." Another stated "financial independence." Yet another expressed "totally in love with one awesome person." Each person's answer seem to reflect their complex value system. For most, the answer was the "one thing that would make them happy for the moment." Yet would it?

The answer that grabbed my attention was one that has taken years for this disciple to realize. One of our elder grandpa's made this statement. "I never realized until recently what a personal relationship is like with the living God."

He grew up in a rule-oriented culture. He didn't experience the grace-based, life-giving life style until several years ago. Now looking back, he is amazed at the quality of life that fills his insides. He now finds it difficult not to express himself from the inside-out. In his early days he measured his life through his toys and achievements. Today it is about a personal relationship with the living King of Kings.

What is the greatest blessing one can receive in this life? What have many Christ-followers discovered? Life's greatest blessing is an intimate, personal relationship with the Triune God. Yes, the same God who created the heavens and earth. The same Being who implemented a plan for human redemption. The identical God who has big plans for humanity in a new age. A relationship built not on a contract but a commitment. Theologians like to name it a covenant. For a covenant is a committed promise between a faithful God and a double-minded humanity. God always fulfills His side of the promise no matter how many times we fail on our side. But more than his promises, the joy of knowing Him and Him knowing us is greater than any promise. Knowing Him is better than heaven, eternal life, or salvation itself.

Yes, when one begins to hang out with the living Triune God, one is blessed. There is no other reason than the joy of the relationship. For knowing God and Him knowing you is the greatest blessing that this life has to offer. Anything else doesn't even compare.

#336 - The Flourishing God

"Who is like you, O Lord, among the gods? Who is like you, majestic in holiness, awesome in glorious deeds, doing wonders?" Exodus 15:11

Have you ever met a person that exudes confidence with humility? sacrificial love with justice? Strength of character with a compassionate attitude for others? I haven't yet met one such human. Yes, there are people with individual traits, but not all three combined together.

As we read the Bible and commune with God, we become more amazed at someone like this. The story of Jesus is such a person. What the writers of the gospels reveal about Him leaves us with an awe of wonder. He not only amazes us, but also gives us a glimpse of who the Father is like. When we look through the frosted lens of our glasses, we then realize why He is God and we are not.

Another attribute that astounds us of God is His life-giving nature. Wherever God goes, whatever He touches, it flourishes. There is a character in the "Lord of The Rings" book version. He never made it into the movie. The author portrayed him as a person who made everything around him to flourish.

The Newsboys also sang a song several years ago entitled "Wherever We Go." Those words showcase how life blooms wherever they went. The grass grows greener. The stock market goes up. The sun shines, and the birds joyfully sing. The imagination only limits what the God-Life must be like.

Our narrow view of God limits us in our understanding of a life that flourishes. Typically in the western world we associate flourishing with personal material gain. Though it is a part, it is a small part. For God, flourishing involves so much more. It is an outer expression of His internal divine nature. It is the standard of who He IS. When he asks humanity to live up to His ways, it is because that is how he lives. It involves healthy, mutual submissive relationships. It emphasizes community along with the individual. Its basis is real love that sacrifices for the sake of others. It emphasis not what is in it for me. But how can we take part with God as He continues His work of completing His plan for humanity.

God wants us to flourish. But, he doesn't want us to perish along the way. For most of us, we are like a rebellious teenager. We want to learn how to drive a car, but lack the maturity and responsibility of our actions. As parents we want them to enjoy more. But providing gifts to early in one's growth may turn deadly for that person and others. Thus, it is best to wait until the proper time.

God is no different with us. His nature is to bless and share His world with others. Yet many of us are not yet ready to handle a life that flourishes. But through time, discipline, and obedience we prove to Him that we are ready. Yet when we are ready, we have most likely matured at a level that it isn't important for us any longer. We are thankful that God in His wisdom knows what is best for us at the right time.

#337 – The Suffering God

"Although he was a son, he learned obedience through what he suffered." Hebrews 5:8

Many people look at suffering as if the person is doing something wrong. In some faith-communities, suffering is viewed as the result of personal sin. Yet when one views the spectrum of the entire Bible one learns that is not true.

First there is Jesus Christ. As the writer of Hebrews states: Jesus learned obedience through what he suffered. Jesus of course never sinned. In the beginning of his ministry, he was led into the wilderness by the Holy Spirit. There He suffered physical exhaustion from lack of food and water. His suffering was not the result of sin, but the deliberate choice of obeying His Father. In his last days, he suffered death on the cross. Again, not because of his sin. But his deliberate choice to fulfill the Godhead's plan of redemption. Jesus stated in John 9:1-3 that a certain blind man was born sightless not because of sin, but for God's glory. The Book of Job 1:1,8 states that God considered Job blameless (sinless) yet his entire world came crumbling down. He suffered physical, emotional, and economic pain. Yes, many religions have difficulty in believing God knows anything personal about suffering. Yet the Incarnation demonstrates what Jesus learned through suffering.

There are those in the Protestant ranks who emphasize the cross without an image of Christ. They claim their focus is on the resurrection. Yet, those in the Catholic faith maintain a statue of a suffering Jesus on the cross. This is their reminder of a suffering Messiah. Both images are correct. Yet one-side likes to focus on one side of the spectrum and ignore the other. The fact is joy and suffering is a part of life.

To enjoy life in Christ is to admit the reality of suffering. Paul wrote in Colossians 1:24 that his suffering is for the benefit of others in the Body of Christ. Yet even in suffering, Paul rejoiced in the Spirit that lived in him and help him through the pain. In I Corinthians 12:26, Paul writes that when one suffers in the Body of Christ, the entire Church suffers. Also, in Acts 9 Jesus is speaking with Paul (then Saul) asking why is he persecuting Him? Paul was persecuting believers, the Body of Christ, not the physical Jesus. Yet Jesus' replied he was personally feeling the pain when the Body of Christ is being attacked.

Isn't it the same when one member suffers within the Body of Christ? When one suffers, isn't Jesus already there in Spirit? Does HE not recall what it was like walking in his physical temple? And as our mediator with the Father, does He now groan with the Spirit for us? Isn't He working out what is best for all parties involved?

Yes, God created life to be enjoyed. Especially when one realizes joy does not come solely from our physical surroundings. But through the Spirit expressing Himself through you. When you know Christ is with you and for you, the more comforting life becomes. And when one learns to trust the Triune God, you wear your pain to glorify HIM.

At the end, we acknowledge our Creator for the faith HE allows us to exercise in those moments of truth. Through suffering, we learn more about Jesus, Father God, and Spirit. We learn endurance. We come to appreciate joy even through our suffering.

#338 - The Enjoyable God

"For he will not much remember the days of his life because God keeps him occupied with joy in his heart." Ecclesiastes 5:20

The more our Triune God reveals Himself to us, the more we bow down in awesome amazement. One theme running through my mind for the past several years is how much life exuberates from His Being.

I grew up in an Eastern European family culture. My parents immigrated from Poland & Ukraine through Germany after WWII. Life during and after the war was no picnic for either of them. The scars of battles, death, and prison camps carried with them for most of their lives. Of course, as parents it rubbed off on the children even though they tried their best to shelter us from the pain. Most of the time is was duty, responsibility, and work that was the number one topic of discussion. It was a rare sight in our household to see laughter and joy expressed.

So when God invited me to join Him on His redemptive mission, I accepted. I then didn't know the cost or sacrifice required. All I knew was what I have been doing wasn't working. In life's journey, this lad began to grow in Christ's grace and knowledge. He began to unlearn old in-grain beliefs and replace them with God's truth. He discovered a new Spirit within him that was never there before. It is God's assurance of HIS work within every believer through the Holy Spirit. As I explored and discovered more about the Triune God, more transformation occurred. You would have seen a greater change in attitude, behavior, and confidence in the Triune God.

What happened over time was the fruit of transformation. This person changed from a quiet introvert to an open, expressive character. He now can't stop to express the love, joy, and faith of life in Christ. The influence of God's Spirit is now like an unstoppable river. The more that comes out and shared with others, the more remains on the inside. It is now like a bottomless churn. It continues to flow without any physical laws of explanation.

Why am I so excited about this? Simply because the more I hang out and walk with God, the more His divine nature presses upon me. His attitude, beliefs, and character rub off on me. The one trait that I marvel more about God than others is the way HE enjoys life. From creation where He said everything He made was "very good." To the resurrection of Christ where the angels rejoiced over the victory of death, sin, and Satan. God enjoys what He does. Jesus himself enjoyed eating and drinking. So much so He was accused for partying with the undesirables of his day.

How much joy does He express when one of His children returns home from their wandering ways? Jesus portrays in the parable of the Prodigal Son a Father running to meet his "lost" son. Afterward he threw a party in celebration of the event.

How often do we walk through life and see "God Events" in the mundane, routine circumstances of the day? What if we took time out and began to count such events on a daily basis? Maybe keep score and turn it into a personal Super Bowl event? When we do, we are reminded of God who created everything as a gift for us to enjoy.

He speaks about Joy in His Word. The fruit of God's Spirit includes Joy. Joy is one of the attributes of who God Is. Most of us take joy for granted. Not I any longer.

#339 - Enjoy Life

"There is nothing better for a person than that he should eat and drink and find enjoyment in his toil. This also, I saw, is from the hand of God, for apart from him who can eat or who can have enjoyment? For to the one who pleases him God has given wisdom and knowledge and joy, but to the sinner he has given the business of gathering and collecting, only to give to one who pleases God." Ecclesiastes 2:24-25

When you look at people in your workplace, home, and neighborhood, how many do you know enjoy life? Or how many are jumping from one activity to another without rejoicing in what they do?

How many people do you know are singing when they work? No, not listen to the music of others, but deep inside rejoice with beautiful (to them) joyful noise?

Doesn't it seem most people we meet have a plastic smile on their face? They force themselves to complete their current task so they can rollover to the next item on their to do list. Then again, what about those people who say IF they had a different job, they would enjoy life more? or if they made more money? or if they were married (or single)? or whatever? Their claim is if they only changed their circumstances, they would definitely then enjoy life more. But would they?

There are many factors that may cause a person to lose their joy, and I am not going to dwell on them. Instead, I am going to shout out my praises today for how to experience my personal favorite: Life in Christ. For most of us this is a religious expression within the Christian culture. For myself, it is the core of life. Life only makes sense when one comes to know who Jesus is. When one accepts who He is, and applies His teachings, one begins to enjoy the process of living. The process leads to freedom and fulfillment. One then comes to experience the adventurous relationship with the Creator God.

When one walks with Him, one acknowledges that his purpose is supreme over any personal plans. And we rejoice that He allows us to participate with Him in His purpose. As we take part with Him, we begin to experience the freedom that comes from serving the King.

He has made us free from the darkness of Satan and the rebellion of godliness. Not only are we free, but amazed at His loving nature and supreme care for each of us. He will pursue us even if one of us leave the 100-fold in pursuit of our personal desires. But more so, after one has an intimate relationship with the Supreme Lover of the universe, who else is there? What else compares? When one reads such scriptures as:

"As for the rich in this present age, charge them not to be haughty, nor to set their hopes on the uncertainty of riches, but on God, who richly provides us with everything to enjoy." 1 Timothy 6:17

"In that day you will ask nothing of me. Truly, truly, I say to you, whatever you ask of the Father in my name, he will give it to you. Until now you have asked nothing in my name. Ask, and you will receive, that your joy may be full." John 16:23-24

"These things I have spoken to you, that my (Jesus) joy may be in you, and that your joy may be full." John 15:11

"The thief comes only to steal and kill and destroy. I (Jesus) came that they may have life and have it abundantly." John 10:10

These are only a few of the scriptures that immediately come to mind.

What if you became a committee of one? And ask our heavenly Father to open the gates of heaven and earth? Ask Him so you may enjoy life the way He created life to be. And as you do so, let His blessings also flow to those you know and meet. Wouldn't that be a wonderful testimony of Kingdom reality as God is glorified? So why not today,

So be radical - Enjoy Life in Christ!

#340 - Joy of the Lord

"Then he said to them, 'Go your way. Eat the fat and drink sweet wine and send portions to anyone who has nothing ready, for this day is holy to our Lord. And do not be grieved, for the joy of the Lord is your strength.'" Nehemiah 8:10

Israel was a nation chosen by God for His purpose to ultimately adopt humanity into the family of God. With Abraham, God began moving history towards His foreordained purpose. From the lineage of Abraham, Isaac, and Jacob, we have the twelve tribes of Israel. That turned into the nation of Israel under Saul, David, and Solomon. Later this led to the birth of Jesus Christ and the redemption of humanity.

So whenever we look at the historical nation of Israel, don't we view our own life through a similar mirror? How often do we look at the Israel nation and shake our head in amazement of their disbelief? And then also question the behavior of their walk with the Lord? Yet if we be honest with ourselves, are we any different?

Around 500 B.C., Nehemiah was a government leader and Ezra the high priest. The nation recently came out of another painful stupor of being disciplined by God. There they rediscovered the Torah. These are the first five books of the Bible written for them. So on this day, the 1st day of their 7 month, they celebrated the Feast of Booths. A celebration of their harvest season. The feast was a seven day event followed by one last great day. The first and last day of the feast were Sabbatical Holy days. The nation on these days would assemble and worship God. This time though the nation rediscovered the Words of God and celebrated. They reconfirmed disciplines they had before stopped conducting. In the midst of their celebration, Nehemiah expressed the concept "the joy of the Lord is our strength." Not Israel's joy. Not Nehemiah's joy. Not anyone's joy but the Lord's.

Does not this imply our Lord has joy He wants to share with others? Doesn't this also imply His joy is stronger and more effective than any joy we may experience apart from him? Also, doesn't this imply that our Lord wants us to experience His joy?

A recent poll revealed that most parents want their children to grow up happy and successful. The poll didn't ask the parents to define happy or successful. But that they wanted the best for their children. Yet many parents have difficulty in separating happiness from joy.

Happiness as many of us old timers discovered is a byproduct of our surrounding world. These may include our circumstances and physical components around us. The challenge is that many of the circumstances needed to be happy are outside of one's control. Most often they are dependent on physical stimulus or expectations that may or may not occur. In other words, happiness is a temporary condition that always seems out-of-our-reach.

But joy is the fruit of the Holy Spirit. A Spirit that supernaturally exudes real, in-depth rejoicing from the inside-out. The Spirit doesn't rely on outside, physical stimulus to celebrate. Instead He simply expresses Himself. Why? Because joy is an attribute of the Triune God. He lives in the soul of a believer.

So when we say our strength is in the joy of the Lord, we acknowledge that God's Spirit resides in us. He empowers us and expresses His life through us. That our courage and backbone is found in Jesus Christ. We celebrate this with the Holy Spirit. We are uplifted by the Creator's own divine nature that flows in us, through us, and from us. As we desist, He increases. As we view life through His eyes, His plans, and His purposes, we rejoice with Him and He rejoices with us. We become one in Spirit and one in Purpose and one in Joy. With such joy, how can one not exercise a strong attribute to glorify God and His people? Is not this the type of joy (and real happiness) we all want?

#341 - Being Aware of Our Need for Jesus Christ

"For you say, I am rich, I have prospered, and I need nothing, not realizing that you are wretched, pitiable, poor, blind, and naked." Revelations 3:17

There are two categories we can place everyone on the planet into. Those who are aware of their need for Jesus Christ and those who are not aware of their need for Jesus Christ. For many of us who have already made a rational decision to follow Jesus, we likewise may fall into either camp. For those who haven't yet made a decision for Christ, you may also fall into either camp. For what separates a person from one camp or the other is not a "decision." But living a life that is "aware of our need" for Jesus Christ 24/7.

What do I mean by being aware of our need? And why Jesus Christ?

Most people view Christianity from the outside-in. They have very little knowledge of its roots, core, or vision. Thus, they disavow its importance in their life. They are self-satisfied with their lot in life and feel they need nothing. They are like the people described in the Book of Revelations (Rev. 3:17). They typically see themselves to be self-sufficient. They believe everything is under control.

How about those raised in a "Christian culture?" Their battle is being overly familiar with Christianity. They may have had a poor model of discipleship to follow. Whatever the situation, the need only arises when confronted with a personal problem. A problem requiring a breakthrough miracle. That miracle many times leads us to become more aware of our need for Jesus Christ.

Most often only when a person comes to the end of themselves are they open to seek answers to life's Big questions. For some it may be survival (ever became lost at sea in the middle of a storm?). For others it may be financial loss (bank accounts empty and no source of income). For some it may be health issues (cancer before age thirty typically starts one to ask questions of life). The death of a love one (facing mortality raises many questions). A breakup of a close, meaningful relationship. The divorce of a trusted friend robbing you of your emotional investment.

Such events stop us to ask those important questions: Is there a God? Who are you God? What do you want from me? Is this all that there is? What is the purpose of life? We begin to ask these questions as we realize that there is a hole within our inner being that needs to be satisfied. There seems to be nothing that we have found on this planet that fills it. Or we realize that life is much bigger than ourselves and we cannot control every facet of it.

Is it possible to have our cup filled and soul replenished? Is it possible to better manage life's situation with the one who is in Control?

So why Jesus Christ?

Many people with greater minds than mine have reached the same conclusion. Jesus Christ and His gospel explains life's most important questions. The answers are not always what we want to hear. But they are answers that explain history and reveal God's purpose. Though many of the details are still a blank page, the plan makes sense. And the spiritual fruit demonstrates its authenticity in the home, marketplace, and community. When allowed to live out, people flourish, find freedom, and fulfillment.

When one studies the life of Jesus Christ and His message, one either accepts His claim or denies it. There is no middle ground. Either Jesus is the divine being who help create the universe or not. Either He chose himself to become human, die, and was resurrected to fulfill Scripture, or not. And He plans on returning as King of Kings, or he is either a liar or a lunatic as C.S. Lewis explained. Either He is the mediator between heaven and earth, or not. Either He is the one person both the Old and New Testaments point too as the Messiah, or not. Again, he is either a liar or a lunatic. When one realizes who He is. When one cannot accept anything less. When one comes to realizes how far we fall short of His Magnificence. When one acknowledges His authority, reign, and purpose in their lives. One receives the assurance of the Holy Spirit.

As we mature, we become a trusted believer that acknowledges Jesus Christ is neither a liar nor a lunatic. He is who He claims to Be.

How aware are you of your need for Jesus Christ in your life?

#342 - Blessed and Broken

"Blessed is the man who makes the Lord his trust, who does not turn to the proud, to those who go astray after a lie!" Psalm:40:4

"The Lord is near to the brokenhearted and saves the crushed in spirit." Palm:34:18

The journey through life contains both moments of satisfaction and times of struggle. Many high school graduates will soon realize this year how unprepared they are to face the world. For them, life is still a fantasy watched through a video screen. Their standards of expectations come from movies and film clips. They watch unknowing each scene is programmed until perfect. They want to experience the ideal, but fail to separate fantasy from reality. The "why not me" mentality confronts them to want more from life than an "average" existence. For most of them, happiness is the goal and money is the prize. Yet for others, survival is the norm and hope is the plan. They are unprepared for the challenges and obstacles to achieve their plan.

Someone once told me at an early age that life consists of blessings and brokenness's. I didn't understand it at the time, but looking back now, I have to agree. Like the caboose on the train track, we are traveling down a path anchored by two rails on both sides of the track. On our left side are the blessings. On our right side are the brokenness's. (Or for others the sides may be switched, but the results are the same). As we travel through life, on any given day, we experience the joy and thrills of victory, meaning, and love. Yet on the same day, even moments apart, we may also experience pain, sorrow, and fear. There is not a person I haven't met who has denied it. Some people may emphasize the blessing more than the brokenness. Others focus on the brokenness more than the blessing. But if they are honest they will admit that both exist at the same time.

As humans, we are all made in the image of God. Yet negatively affected by our alienation from God. We all have experience heavenly and hellish moments. The real question is which side are we going to emphasize in our life? For most of us, our human condition wants to control the environment around us. We are fearful to trust a living God. So, we focus on trying to manage (plan, organize, and control) the broken side of life.

Others though have come to learn to place their brokenness into the hands of a Jesus. There His divine nature redeems, restores, and blesses us. The broken-side treats others as the enemy. The blessed-side relates with others as God's children. We are included in Jesus Christ. But blind from the ignorance and destructive spiritual forces. The broken-side uses and manipulates others for their personal agenda. The blessed-side paints a vision of options. Then lets others decide which is best for them and their community. The broken-side takes all they can get for themselves. The blessed-side gives to others without any expectation of a return. The broken-side pities themselves while blaming others. The blessed-side thanks their Provider. They also pray that others may come to know Him. Through all life's journey, the blessed-side realizes how blessed they are. Why? Because God carries us through our brokenness.

We have learned to acknowledge our brokenness and allow God's Spirit to regenerate us. We know who our Savior is. We don't deny or hide from our brokenness. Instead we like Paul acknowledge that when we are weak, then God is strong in us. For that we are thankful and realize how truly blessed we are.

How about you? What ways has God taken your brokenness and blessed you? Or blessed others through you?

#343 - Thievery Against Marriage

"Let marriage be held in honor among all, and let the marriage bed be undefiled, for God will judge the sexually immoral and adulterous." Hebrews 13:4

Marriage has been under attack from day one. Our first example is Adam & Eve. Eve began to spend more time listening to the serpent rather than commune with Adam and the Lord. The result was a global catastrophe. The temptation of grabbing the non-compliant fruit turned into a path of alienation. Humanity still struggles from the impact.

Jesus himself stated from the beginning God created the marriage relationship. One man with one woman (Mark 10:6-9) begot the marriage institution. Yet mankind's stony heart could not understand nor follow God's intention for marriage. So through the Bible He reveals how mankind is to behave toward Himself and others for our own sake.

The marriage relationship pictures the relationship between the church and Christ. The relationship is built with sacrificial love. Empowered by mutual submission. Plus a lifelong commitment of faithfulness. It pictures the same relationship Father God, Son, and Holy Spirit have with one another.

In many ways, the covenantal marriage provides a safe haven for two people. The institution allows you to experience the abundant relational life that God enjoys. But when two people are in a contractual arrangement, than marriage is only a business. Two people satisfying each other needs in exchange for services rendered. What type of marriage relationship would you prefer?

God reveals the type of behavior and attitude that leads to a prosperous marriage. His Word highlights what builds-up and what breakdowns the marriage relationship. They include external and internal factors.

Here are some external factors that destroy marriage. They include adultery, incest, same-sex relationships, pornography, and fornication. Internal factors include non-submissiveness, selfishness, and ungodliness. All these factors are thieves of marriage blissfulness. The following are Biblical texts that highlight marriage relationship builders. Ephesians 5; 1 Corinthians 7; and Hebrews 13:4.

Marriage is the ideal place for two people to enjoy the same relationship of the Triune God. Yet, as always, mankind wants to take shortcuts. They want the personal benefits at the expense of the community. God's way may hurt a few upfront in the beginning of the process. But leads to long term success and riches for the majority as well as the few.

It takes trust to know that the eternal values of God always lead to the best outcome in the long run. Marriage is no different. So if we want to enjoy a rich relationship that marriage brings, than let us begin. How? By personally standing up as a committee of one. By voicing our disapproval whenever we notice thievery against marriage. By simply witnessing what marriage pictures in our daily life. And if necessary, use words.

#344 - Who Do You Trust?

"In God I trust; I shall not be afraid. What can man do to me?" Psalm 56:11

Trust is built within relationships. Without relationships, trust wouldn't matter. Trust is important. Why? Because it brings two or more parties together toward a mutual destination.

If you ever been on a team, or served in the armed forces, than you know the importance of building trust among others. If you are in serious relationship as a husband and wife, than you know. If you are in a healthy nurturing relationship between parent and child, than you know. Or if you are in an accountability relationship between an employer and employee, you likewise know.

Within all these relationships, we have tasted the fruit of trust. The fruit may have tasted sour at times. But I'm sure in-between you have also tasted the sweetness of a trustful relationship. Most likely there is or was one person that allowed you to experience the savory joy of trusting another. Yet, during that same period there were probably many others that caused you to distrust. So you kept them at an arm's distance away from the heart.

For most of us, learning to trust our Triune God is a time investment. It requires commitment and obedience without focusing on immediate results. The Book of Hebrews (11) summarizes many people of faith who held on in trust of God without receiving a reward in this life. In fact, many of them lost everything including their life in a hideous manner. Yet they trusted God to the very end.

When someone asks me today how do I measure success in this life, my reply is one word: Trust. Real success is not how many toys one accumulates in this life. It is not how famous or important one becomes in the eye of others. It is not necessarily experiencing life's good things. Though a blessed marriage, career, and meaningful relationships are a part.

At the end of our life, Jesus is going to review our relationship with Him. Our life is either going to exemplify trust in our self or in Him. He is going to review through the trials, tests, and moments of truth how much we trusted Him. Sought Him. Followed Him. He will reward us. He is also going to measure how well we submitted to the Holy Spirit's lead in our life, and likewise reward us.

Yes we are saved by Jesus' life, death, and resurrection. But, the Bible also teaches we are rewarded by how we grow in our daily interaction with Him and each other.

So the next time someone asks you how do you measure success in life, maybe your answer will be like mine. I trust in Jesus Christ.

#345 - If You Are Spiritual, Whose Spirit Do You Follow?

"Beloved, do not believe every spirit, but test the spirits to see whether they are from God, for many false prophets have gone out into the world." 1 John 4:1

One of the most often cultural feedback's I get now-a-days is: "I'm not into religion; I'm into spirituality." When that phrase comes at me look out, I get overly excited. Why? Because either God's Spirit is working in the mind of the person or I have met someone who may be open to something much greater.

My first reply is generally a question that goes something like this. "Great, so am I; tell me, whose Spirit do you follow?" Depending on the reply, we have many options to choose. The fact is I have the opportunity to develop a relationship with a future adoptive child of God. Generally, we get several different types of responses.

We may get anything from "I follow Jesus Christ through the leadership of the Holy Spirit." All the way to the other extreme. "I study the movement of the stars in relationship with my pet snake under a red moon." Most often the comments come somewhere between. The response doesn't matter. It allows me to start building a relationship. And if they want to know more, I am always open to witness Jesus Christ and His Spirit with others.

When one learns to communicate Scripture into an everyday meaningful message, people listen. This allows one to share the gospel from their perspective. For example, when others are open to the spiritual world, it is easier to explain the importance of being influenced by the most powerful Spirit. Then we can compare the Holy Spirit with anything they present.

This is where it is fun to share one's life experience with your testimony. No one can deny your experience of being transformed from the inside-out by the Holy Spirit. Especially if you reflect Jesus Christ in your life. They will see how you exemplify the real love, joy, and peace that comes from such a heavenly relationship. When you isolate which spirit the other person is attuned too, allows you to boast of the real fruit of the Holy Spirit.

As a believer and faith monger, we all have stories and examples to share of people who have made the transition from a dead spirit to a living Godly Spirit.

So the next time someone says that they are into spirituality, jump at the chance to share with them you walk with the best Spirit of them all – The Holy Spirit!

#346 - Witchcraft in the Marketplace

"As we were going to the place of prayer, we were met by a slave girl who had a spirit of divination and brought her owners much gain by fortune-telling." Acts 16:16

Most people's concept of witchcraft makes them think of potions, wands, and black pointed hats. Usually these tools are being used by ugly women with a bitter facial expression. You may recall witches from such movies as "Harry Potter and ...." or "Wizard of Oz." For most of us, witches are a make believe fantasy. Yet, God's word recommends us to stay away from them (Deut. 18:10). Are they for real or have witches gone away along with the devil in red underwear and pitchfork?

The Bible most often uses the word sorcerer to identify those who practice wizardry. They are people who create harmful illusions, or play with unholy spirits. They point others away from trusting the Triune God. Their base of operation is built on falsehood. The Bible gives unpleasant examples of sorcerers and their outcomes. There is Pharaoh & Moses (Ex7:11), Daniel & the Chaldean King (Dan 2:2), and Micah's prophecy of the end times (Mic. 5:12). The Book of Revelations likewise mentions what becomes of sorcerers at the end of the age (Rev 22:15).

What does sorcery look like in the marketplace? It comes in many forms but here are a few examples. 1) The illusion of success built on the back of others. For example, a sales brochure cover of a twenty-story office building. But one only rents desk space. 2) The distorted numbers of monthly reports. Separate financial statements for different agencies is a good example. Also reports built on estimates but treated as actual. 3) Keeping two sets of books.

One the public sees and the other telling the true picture [Enron]). 4) Building a business organization through a Ponzi scheme. You find this most often within the investment community. There the players must get money from new investors to payout previous investors. (examples too many to mention.) 5) Portraying the ideal through media and advertisement. (e.g. glamor magazine touch-ups). 6) Happiness through materialism (name your favorite product). 7) Dress for success (focus on form rather than substance). 8) Lies in advertisement (we see this come alive in political campaigns). The list is endless.

What witchcraft sells is falsehood. Witchcraft denies accountability to a final Judge. It removes God from the picture, and pushes for personal agendas no matter what the cost or price. It places the outcome and means more important than people, truth, and God's sovereign plan. In the end, it is a lie that hurts and destroys individuals, families, and institutions. It is generally self-centered. It does not take into consideration the full ramifications or impact of others. It prevents people from having an authentic relationship with God and people. It destroys character, damages eternal values, and ruins lives in the process.

As faith-builders, we are called to restore God's Kingdom reign in the marketplace. It begins with one person's commitment to follow the lead of the Holy Spirit in business. It begins with you and me.

So next time when you see witchcraft within the workplace, diplomatically call it out. Provide a better solution built on principles of honesty, truth, and authenticity. Your clients, supervisors, and peers may disagree with you. But at least you have taken a stand for Christ and those around you. In the end, your example may lead others along with you toward the real promise land.

#347 - How Do Idols Hurt You?

"You shall have no other gods before me." Deuteronomy 5:6-8

When God gave the Ten Commandments, He gave specific instructions that would benefit humanity. One of those instructions was to refrain from worshiping other gods. We have come to know these other gods as idols.

Now some of us may think God is a jealous Being who does not tolerate us worshiping someone more than Him. Some may look at this commandment from a religious aspect. Or how do I keep it to receive blessings from God. Others may look at it from an obedience perspective. Which means we only do it without contemplating the impact toward others. Some may even search the Bible looking for a way to get around observing the rule. In other circles, God is believed to be an ego centrist Being. He wants total domination over His creation. He along insists total adherence to all the rules so He may better control us. There are more viewpoints. These are only a few.

The plain truth of the matter though is God realizes if we don't have a direct relationship with Him, we suffer. He knows without Him; we are failing to live our potential. When we pursue a lie, we eventually hurt ourselves and the people around us. Instead of dealing with reality, idols drown us to live in a fantasy world. They will boomerang and hit us on the side of the head when we least expect it. Typically, they are a false, short term substitute for the real thing.

For the record, idols are anything that comes between you and God. It is what we want now and cannot wait for God's timetable. It becomes our main focus, drive, and passion. We worship and adore them instead of the living God. They give the false illusion of temporary satisfying our inner desires. It is something that has a hold of our heart and doesn't allow the Triune God to lead the way. The end result leads to treading outside of His Will. When we live outside of His Will, we are on our own. Yes it may work out for the short term; and yes you may even blossom from it for the short term. But over time the sour taste of sin and godliness will emerge. The outcome will not be as rich and abundant for all stakeholders as you first thought.

Many of us eventually learn that idols are a poor substitution for the Triune God. The more we seek to walk with the real God, the stronger our faith becomes. The more confidence we have in God, the less temporary pleasures and escapes we seek from idols. We become like the Thessalonians Paul writes about in Chapter 1:9. "... and how you turned to God from idols to serve the living and true God."

Yes, when one places the true God as the sole center in everything we do, idols lose their luster. So the sooner one removes the handcuffs of idols, the quicker one experiences the enriching relationship with the Triune God.

So, what idols are preventing you from walking in step with the Spirit? What are you going to do about it?

#348 - Religiosity

"For I tell you, unless your righteousness exceeds that of the scribes and Pharisees, you will never enter the kingdom of heaven." Matt. 5:20

When one reviews the Bible, it seems the people God had the greatest animosity against were the "religious people." This was true from the Old Testament patriarchs to the New Testament saints. They would rile God's emotions to a tilt. The reason? Because they prevented others from having an authentic, meaningful relationship with Him.

Jesus' encounter with the Pharisees is a prime example. "But woe to you, scribes and Pharisees, hypocrites! For you shut the kingdom of heaven in people's faces. For you neither enter yourselves nor allow those who would enter to go in." (Matt. 23:13). Here Jesus explodes with a verbal assault aimed directly at the Pharisees. They had become so self-righteous they maintained a form of religion, but lack the power and love of God with it (2 Corinthians 5:12). They blinded themselves with a humanistic show of piety but the heart didn't know God. They acted the part in form, but lacked the internal substance of genuine love. Whereas King David was a man after God's own heart [Acts 13:22], the Pharisees were men after their idol's heart.

The apostle Paul also wrote in Romans 16:18. "For such persons do not serve our Lord Christ, but their own appetites, and by smooth talk and flattery they deceive the hearts of the naive." Throughout Paul's ministry the struggle was with people who were deceived into worshipping idols rather than the true God. For whatever one set's their heart after, that is not submitted under the

Triune God, is pursuing what the Bible defines as an idol. And idols have their followers and supporters even in the 21st century.

Religiosity is the idol of mystical performance. It looks sacred from the outside-in, but lacks the Spirit-filled heart that knows and walks with God from the inside-out. Religiosity is the friend of humanism. It is designed to make man feel good, look good, and for a moment experience good. But the end result is another deceptive lie which eventually leads to more anxiety and pain.

Jesus spoke about having a deep, meaningful relationship with Him. He didn't act religious. Instead He invited others to be involved with Him. They became His family, community, and government built from the center of God's heart.

His way is about everyday life; not a one-hour religious experience. It is expressing the love of God with your family members, work associates, and neighbors. The unity is not found in a bunch of do's and don'ts [Col. 2:20], but in the Spirit of God within each person.

At the end of the day, one finds having a relationship with Jesus Christ is an adventurous journey. Sharing life with Him has all the excitement of a Hollywood blockbuster movie. The difference though is you are not a spectator but an active participant in the plot and storyline. He assigns you a role that you were specifically designed to live and equips you for its fulfillment. It is about everyday life. When you eat, sleep, work, play, dance, sing, write, love and yes lead and serve others, you are reflecting Him.

When one discovers and experiences this way of life, one understands why Jesus became angry with the religious people of His day. You may want to take a hard look at oneself and ask in prayer. What religious games can we stop playing so we may draw closer to the living God and share more of His way with others?

#349 - Because I Can

"I can do all things through him who strengthens me." Philippians 4:13

This morning I biked approximately twenty miles. When asked why I do it, my reply is straight forward, "because I can." My wife mowed the lawn this past week. When our neighbors asked how come I don't do it or hire it out, my reply again is straight forward, "because she can." When you asked my friend Frank, a paraplegic, why he rides his motorized wheel chair from his apartment to the local tavern one mile away for a beer, he replies "because I can."

Now someone else asked me the other day how come I don't play professional racquetball. My reply, "because I can't." Time has passed up the season when I would have been able. Today, I simply play for pleasure; "because I can."

A couple of weeks ago, a friend was involved in an auto accident. He was riding a motorbike safely following traffic regulations, only one mile from his home, when a person drove her car through an intersection right into him. She claimed she didn't see him. After multiple surgeries, the medical team believes he will walk again. However, the physical rehab is going to be long and strenuous. There is much he will miss this year - and in many cases his "because I can" opportunities will be limited. Yet as he states, there are things he will continue to do "because he can."

As Christ-followers, we are blessed with the living God residing in us. As we desist and He increases, our faith, trust, and hope in Him is strengthen. We find ourselves listening more to his instructions and directions. We develop confidence in Him and look forward to the opportunities of living life for His glory.

Every time we express a godly attribute, we recognize him more and more. Every time we accept a new challenge, or take another adventurous journey with Him, our confidence and trust in Him becomes a force that breaks down fears, lies, and human pride. We find ourselves doing activities that are outside our normal sphere. When asked why, our reply is straight forward "because I can."

#350 - Happy Birthday!

"When a woman is giving birth, she has sorrow because her hour has come, but when she has delivered the baby, she no longer remembers the anguish, for joy that a human being has been born into the world." John 16:21

When the day of your birth rolls around another year, how do you celebrate it? Do you throw yourself a party? Do you invite a few friends over for dinner? Or are you fortunate to have friends or family members that throw a party on your behalf?

However you celebrate your birthday, you may want to consider this: you didn't give birth, but your mother did. So on your next birthday, why not take an intentional moment and celebrate your birth with the person who gave birth - your mother. In other words, technically it is not your birthday, but your Mother's.

The other person you may want to thank and celebrate the day with is the Author of life, the Triune God. Without Him, you and I would not be here today. In fact, He gives us life, breath, and purpose. We are not accidents, but planned living souls designed for His pleasure for all eternity. It all begins on the day your Mother gave birth and continues with His divine intervention on a daily basis.

So when your day comes, stop, thank your Mother, and celebrate your adventurous journey rooted in Jesus Christ with the Author of Life. What other way is better than this to celebrate and rejoice on your Birthday?

#351 - Want to Become A More Effective Christ-Follower?

"But grow in the grace and knowledge of our Lord and Savior Jesus Christ." 2Peter 3:18

Last week heard another message of how to live the transformed life. I have lost count of how many of these messages keep repeating the same theme. Beginning to wonder if this is one of the causes why the Christian community struggles to impact today's culture.

If someone keeps selling you the importance of doing more, instead of allowing God to become more involved in your life. Stop. Doing more from a humanistic perspective is not the answer. Why than is God even necessary? Yes, studying your Bible is good. Using your talents and gifts to serve others is God's way. Cultivating relationships is important. But whether those around become "saved" is not your responsibility. Jesus has that under control. All these activities are good. But let's not emphasize doing more from a humanistic perspective. Instead, let's work with God. Maybe, HE expects something else from us.

Again the bullet points from the minister were very good. But, as usual they emphasized one person's narrow perspective. One question always seem to arise during these messages. Why doesn't the minister just preach what the Bible says? We are referring to 2 Peter which main purpose is to highlight how a person can live a fruitful life in Christ.

The author of 2 Peter emphasizes the main reason for his letter is to encourage you "to grow in the grace and knowledge of Jesus Christ." Chapters one and two outline the details. In chapter 1:3-8 we are instructed how to build our faith (trust). By practicing love, brotherly affection, godliness, steadfastness, self-control, knowledge, and virtue. When we pursue these values, we will increase in spiritual fruit and effectiveness. Why? Because these traits reflect the character of God.

What many of us eventually come to learn about the transformed life is the focus becomes "more about God and less about us." When Paul wrote "we can do all things through Christ who strengthens us," he was emphasizing Christ and de-emphasizing you and me.

Which leads us to the question: Is not the best way to know anyone is by living with them? When we share life with someone don't we come to know who and what they believe and how they approach life? Is not this the same with our Lord? Is not when we study about the life of Jesus Christ, who He is, what he did, and what he plans to do, we come to know him better. And the more we hang out with him, don't we likewise come to know him better? Don't we grow as we walk through life and experience his grace upon us? And as we live in Him and as He lives in us, don't we grow in His grace and develop a more intimate relationship with Him?

It seems what we really need to learn is how to love Him with all our heart, mind, body, and strength. When we do, don't we begin to experience the fruit of His Spirit? Is not then when we step back and realize how we are being transformed into His image not by what we do, but by what He is doing? The truth dare to be told. We hang on to Him knowing the best is yet to come.

#352 - Sin: Problem or Symptom?

"No one who abides in him keeps on sinning; no one who keeps on sinning has either seen him or known him." 1 Jn. 3:6

As an independent consultant, I am called upon to help solve problems. Sometimes the problem is easy to identify and a solution implemented. Other times, the problem is cloudy by all the smoke. The biggest challenge is to refocus the client's thinking. Most of the time people focus on symptoms rather than the actual cause.

For example, if you are having a cash flow problem, is that the actual problem or the symptom of something deeper? Like not having a job or income stream. Many of us will focus on the symptom - no money, rather than on the actual problem - no job. Isn't sin like that?

In our early walk with the Lord, we want to remove sin from our life. So we adhere to the Ten Commandments. We read our Bibles to find out all the do's and don'ts. Then find ourselves frustrated when the results are negligible. It has taken many of us many years to learn that sin is not the problem, but the symptom. The real problem is an absence of an intimate relationship with the Living God.

The depth and intimacy of your relationship with the Triune God will determine the impact sin has on your life. When we have a strong desire to walk with Him. Where His divine character expresses itself in us and through us. Where we know He lives in us. We will then find ourselves yielding more and more to Him. Sin will become a minor hiccup in your life.

Though sin will still impact you. But you will find God's grace an overflowing aroma to lessen sins blows toward you.

C.S. Lewis once wrote that we don't learn to be Christ-followers. We catch it. Like a good virus it impregnates us and grows in us. The more we hang out and come to know God (not just know about Him) the more we enjoy Him and learn from Him. We surrender ourselves and follow the King of Kings via the Holy Spirit that lives in us.

It is not about emphasizing the removal of sin from our life. But more importantly, it's about having a strong, intimate relationship with our King. As you allow Him to live in you, you will reflect His ways. You will refrain from temptations to keep your relationship of trust intact.

When we live a Christ-centric life, our love, joy, and peace comes from Him. As He blesses us, we express the same blessing toward others. Again, sin is not the problem, but only the symptom. A close, intimate relationship with the Living God is a great defense against the temptation of sin. When we are daily infatuated and memorized by His love, we run away from sin's darkness to swim in his wonderful light.

So next time we find our self on the wrong side of sin's darkness, you may want to ask yourself these questions. Did I really submit to God's heart on the matter or just followed my natural desire to please myself? How deep and strong is my current relationship with the Triune God? Am I walking with God or am I trying to make God walk with me? What are you going to do about it?

#353 - Four Godly Attributes of a Successful Business

"For what does it profit a man if he gains the whole world and loses or forfeits himself?" Luke 9:25

The book *Great Business Emulates a Good God* is the outcome of my doctoral dissertation. This case study highlighted four characteristics found in business organizations. These organizations were categorized either as faith focused, friendly, or neutral. The difference between these three categories is the weight placed on the importance of faith in the workplace.

The four characteristics are: 1) faithfulness in relationships. 2) excellence in performance. 3) fruitful in results. 4) integrity in action. The six case studies show how each characteristic is a key value of their business and an attribute of the Triune God.

It did not matter if the business was Christ-centered or neutral in relationship with Jesus. It did not take into account the motive, heart, or allegiance of the organization. It simply focused on these eternal values within the business context.

So if your business only measures profit metrics, maybe it's time to change. How about measuring the relationships of customers, employees, and vendors? What metrics do you use to measure work quality? How engaged are your employees? How fulfilled are your people in your mission objectives? How do you elevate the importance of integrity? You may be surprised by the results.

One recent Harvard study showed about 47% of an organization's bottom-line is the result of its culture. If something impacts almost 50% of the bottom-line, shouldn't we measure and focus on its performance?

Then again, when the Spirit of Christ is alive in the hearts of employees, maybe measuring is not as important. What do you think?

#354 - Is Your Jesus Dead or Alive?

"And if Christ has not been raised, your faith is futile and you are still in your sins." 1 Corinthians 15:17

Easter is the time Christianity comes together to celebrate the resurrection of Jesus Christ. We in the faith may argue whether He died and was buried for a full three days and three nights as He prophesied. Or whether they were portions of three days and nights.

We may also argue among ourselves in regards to the symbolism of the bread and wine. Whether the bread is actually His body or simply a symbol of His human sacrifice. We may also debate whether communion is an institutional doctrine of the church only to be taken in a church service. Or may the bread and wine also be taken at family meal time. Weren't these items standard staples within the middle-eastern cultural meal? Either way, Jesus instructed us to take them and recall His sacrifice and future return.

No matter the discussions and disagreements, there is one universal truth among believers. Jesus arose from the grave and lives today!

He didn't arise and simply disappear into heaven for His sake. He is now at the right hand of God the Father. He now intervenes for humanity before our great God. He is working through the hands and feet of His body, the universal Church. He is preparing a people for His return.

The Bible describes a one-thousand year reign when Christ and His Kingdom will be visible. A time of preparation for a new heaven and a new earth to finally merge together with God's throne among the people for all to see.

How many people do you know live their life with a dead Christ rather than a living Messiah? Does not Jesus become more real as we live out our faith each day? Does not HE become more real as we trust the Spirit to lead us into a deeper relationship with the living God?

Yet if we try to live out the Christian life alone, thinking Jesus is dead and not coming back, doesn't that leave one struggling with a dead faith?

Easter is a time to reflect on what Christ did, is doing, and will be doing as He moves history toward the restoration of all things. My prayer is all may come to know and allow Jesus Christ to express Himself freely through us all.

#355 - Bless My Business

"Thus says the Lord, your Redeemer, the Holy One of Israel: 'I am the Lord your God, who teaches you to profit, who leads you in the way you should go.'" Isaiah 48.17

How many business operations do you know actually glorify God in their service to others? How many of those are operated or owned by believers? How many are controlled by non-believers. But their work exemplifies quality of godliness? These questions challenged me when I completed my dissertation. The final results ended up in a book entitled "Great Business Emulates a Good God."

One of the items to surprise me the most was how many non-Christian business operations practiced godly principles. Also others who exercised eternal values that magnified the qualities of the Triune God. Yet the main difference between the two pertained to motive. Christian-focused business' operated to glorify God. Faith-neutral operations focused on glorifying their brand. Yet both sides operate businesses the world would say were successful. At least from the outside looking in.

Why bring up these facts? Because many of us want and desire God's favor on our business. But sadly still operate with self-centered motives. We want God's blessings, but refrain from being honest with Him in our dealings with others. We haven't yet come to a place where we have surrendered the entire business under the domain of King Jesus.

How do you know if you have surrendered the business to God's domain? Ask yourself, what is the foundation of your business? Why are you in business? Do you actually operate under Kingdom economic principles or follow the ways of the world? Do you practice decision-making that benefits ALL stakeholders of the enterprise? That means partners, employees, vendors, lenders, government agencies, and investors. Do you actually seek God's will before making key decisions that impact the business' mission? Does the business' mission include glorifying God in word and action? Is one of your highest values to serve the common good of others with profit secondary? Are you on a crusade to promote the well-being of all parties, or simply too benefit a few insiders?

These are tough questions. But how can one expect to be blessed if one is conducting business outside of God's character, nature, or will? The transition doesn't happen overnight. But God is merciful. If our heart is open he will lead us to the economic promise land. For most of us, it is a process of repentance, change, and redirecting our hearts to see the world as He does. And even though we may fall far short from perfection, God rewards and blesses those that walk with Him. Yes, catch His vision for your life and business. But more so, learn to rest in the favor of God and His graceful blessings.

#356 - How About Blessing Those You Are With?

"In all things I have shown you that by working hard in this way we must help the weak and remember the words of the Lord Jesus, how he himself said, 'It is more blessed to give than to receive.'" Acts 20:35

Someone once made the comment that if you have something to share with others, than you are actually one blessed person. In doesn't mean you are super wealthy. It only means that you have more than you actual need at the moment.

In fact, having something to share may be more than just material items. It may also include time, words, compassion, encouragement, hope, and maybe even a listening ear.

Have you ever considered our God is in the blessing business?

So how about partnering with Him with the people around you at this very moment? What can you say or do to bless those around you at this very moment? What can you say or do to bless those you meet during the day? What can you say or do to bless those who come within ten feet of you today?

Before you begin, ask God to lead you. Ask Him who you can be a blessing for at least one person this day? Then one new person every day for one week? Afterward, you will experience what Jesus meant when he said it is more blessed to give than receive (Acts 20:35). When you join Him, you will begin to experience the joy of serving Him through others.

#357 - How Do You Measure Success?

"Then I saw a new heaven and a new earth, for the first heaven and the first earth had passed away, and the sea was no more. And I saw the holy city, new Jerusalem, coming down out of heaven from God, prepared as a bride adorned for her husband. And I heard a loud voice from the throne saying, "Behold, the dwelling place of God is with man. He will dwell with them, and they will be his people, and God himself will be with them as their God. He will wipe away every tear from their eyes, and death shall be no more, neither shall there be mourning, nor crying, nor pain anymore, for the former things have passed away." Rev. 21:1-4

In the business world, everything that is important and valued is measured. We track and evaluate data, processes, and systems for constant improvement. But in our personal walk with the Triune God, do we do the same? If so, how do you measure your relationship with our Lord?

For example, when you view the world's religious landscape, what do you notice?

- There are those who place emphasis on keeping rules.

- There are those who emphasize a specific denomination.

- There are those who observe special days.

- There are those who place minor trust in Jesus and make something else the major.

- There are those who place trust in their ability to do good work.

- There are those who place trust in their service toward others.

- There are those who place trust in pursuing causes for social justice.

- There are those who place trust in maintaining a loving relationship with others.

- There are those who place trust in yoga, karma, or the cosmos.

- There are those who place trust in their ability to recall scripture.

- There are those who place trust in attending church services on a regular basis.

- There are those who place trust in participating in local, Christian fellowship.

- There are those who place trust in observing unique rituals.

- There are those who place trust in their ability to pray.

- There are those who place trust...(add your own observation)

The point is many of us place trust everywhere but in Jesus. Yet, trusting His claim as Savior, Lord, and King from our heart, head, and will in everyday life's circumstances is all we really have to claim. A total, dependent trust that His life, death, and resurrection gives us birth unto a new life. A life that we can taste now. A hope that we can believe.

The real measure of spiritual success is our faith (trust) in Him. No matter the trial. No matter the situation. No matter the challenge we face. Our faith is constantly being tested and strengthen through the circumstances of life. Though we may fail to live up to our expectations, He is committed to being faithful and will complete the task. We just need to hang in there with Him.

The fact is Jesus knows our human condition. Most of the time we are discovering where we really do stand before God, and it's not pretty. I am one believer who is very thankful Jesus is my judge and jury and He includes us within His story. We are simply his servants enjoying the ride.

How goes your trust in Jesus? He himself wondered whether there would be real, trusting faith in this world when he returns (Luke 18:8). Yet, no matter where you stand, Jesus loves you and enjoys you becoming more like HIS heavenly Father. He desires your involvement with HIM. HE is looking to build mutual trust with you. In return, HE is willing to invest heaven's resources for your successful life journey unto heaven's promise land. Heaven on earth is the goal. There is no real success until then.

#358 - What Do You Mean Ask, Seek, Knock?

"Ask and it will be given to you; seek and you will find; knock and the door will be opened to you. For everyone who asks receives; the one who seeks finds; and to the one who knocks, the door will be opened." Luke 11:9-10 (NIV)

When Jesus stated the principle of asking, seeking, and knocking, HE was speaking about receiving good from God. This included the presence of the Holy Spirit in one's life. Over the years, I have come to learn the same principle after praying. I now expect my prayers to be answered. Why? Because God is Good. The answer may not be the one I want or prefer, but when we pray seeking God's Will the answer is very livable. Whether yes, no, or not yet, one appreciates HIS involvement in our micro-plans.

The paradigm for prayer is to focus on asking, seeking and knocking for an answer. Yet, how often have we *asked* our Heavenly Father for help in a matter and then sat back and waited. When nothing happens, we wonder how come God didn't answer our prayers.

We need to learn from God's creation. For example, how does God provide food on a daily basis for birds? We need to learn the art of leaving the nest to *seek* the answer. Yes, God provides food for birds. But the bird must leave the comfort of their nest and *seek* for it. We need to do likewise.

The principle of *knocking* is one that I have also recently begun to understand. For many years, I would come to the doorway of opportunity and knock. If the door opened slightly, I would then exercise all the strength and tools at my disposal to manipulate the door wider. This was especially true if it was something that I really wanted.

Now, I come to the door, knock, and wait for it to open. I don't force it. I don't push. I don't seek influential help from others to open it. I patiently wait for God to open the door for me. What have I discovered? When I wait unto the Lord, the door opens from the other side without my influence. The entire passageway thereafter is a blessing all the way through to the other end. It's like dominoes falling down with very little effort. Otherwise if it is not meant to be, I'm OK with it. I will then move-on and continue to seek HIS answer.

So next time you *ask* your Heavenly Father for something, keep *seeking* for the answer. And when you come up to the door of opportunity, *wait for the Spirit to open it*. You will be pleasantly surprised by the results. In the end our Great God, not us, is glorified. And likewise, we walk away learning to trust HIM more and more while favorably experiencing the joy of Kingdom living.

#359 – Lonely Hearts

"You shall have no other gods before Me." Exodus 20:3

Ever sat in a room with hundreds of people and felt alone? Ever spent an evening with a person who you enjoyed being with yet still felt disconnected? Ever wonder how come the person you are married too doesn't fill the empty hole in your heart?

What's missing?

Most of us look for love and fulfillment on a vertical sphere. If not satisfied, we change partners, careers, locations, and even clothes. We think a change will fill up our inner cup.

Yet each may satisfy for the short term. But over time the feeling disappears and we look for something else to change. These are the "gods" in our life. They are generally good things, but by themselves they are incomplete.

So if this is you, do you think it might be time to change your perspective? Instead of chasing vertical relationships and material consumption, how about refocusing? Why not add horizontal connections into your life.

Many of my associates did and acknowledged the vast improvement in their relationships. When the Triune God became their center, they found satisfaction, meaning, and fulfillment. They admit reaching upward before stretching vertical made everything else fall into place. They like me failed to find their emotional cups full until we found our home in Christ Jesus.

Today, He via the Holy Spirit fills our inner longings. Most times without us even realizing or many times not even asking. God knows what we need and what tickles our fancy. So HE being generous fills our joy with cups overflowing without us even asking. HE does for our sake and to share with others. He creates in us everything we lack. He lives in community with himself and enjoys sharing His experiences with us all. When he is the center of everything, everything becomes more satisfying and fulfilling.

He created everything for our long-term enjoyment. Yet without him, the same people, things, and events are empty. With Him, life adds more color, deeper meaning, and emotional connection. Until you experience life with God, you never know what you are missing. You are never lonely again, for He lives in you and will be with you, your entire life.

With Him, you may find yourself alone, but you are never lonely. He is always with you; and you know that you know which allows you to live out what you know. You know what I mean? Probably not, unless you know.

#360 - With God or Without God?

...remember that you were at that time separated from Christ, alienated from the commonwealth of Israel and strangers to the covenants of promise, having no hope and without God in the world. Eph. 2:12 '

Are you aiming too low?

Dallas Willard, author and minister, passed away last year. I for one truly enjoyed his work and will miss him. He was blessed with insight to take Biblical concepts and make them practical for us non-theologians.

One of his concepts was to explain life as "the with-God life." A life centered in Christ and experienced through the Holy Spirit. The opposite would be a life apart from God. So in reflecting, I wrote below a few reasons why I enjoy the with-God life.

- With God we enjoy His blessings; apart from God we wait for luck.

- With God we experience His divine nature; apart from God we are along with our human limitations.

- With God we catch His Life; apart from God we are taught life.

- With God we are found in Christ; apart from God we are lost in Christ.

- With God we are comforted by his Spirit; apart from God we are left on our own.

- With God we have purpose for life; apart from God, we act like an accidental blip that evolved from cosmic dust.

- With God we realize our divine design; apart from God, we strive to make ourselves unfulfilled.

- With God we discover wholesomeness; apart from God, we are never satisfied.

- With God we participate in his Story; apart from God, we mess up our lines.

- With God we have hope; apart from God, we walk plagued by fear.

- With God we learn to love; apart from God, we are painfully lonely.

- With God we are fully alive; apart from God, we are dead people walking.

You may notice, I have a bias toward enjoying life with God. How about you? What else would you add to the above list?

About the Author

After stewarding senior leadership roles with several national organizations, Mike now serves as an adjunct professor with a local faith-based university, active with Stephen Ministry, and facilitates small groups within his faith community. He holds a PhD in pastoral ministry and a graduate degree in management.

His passion is to engage, encourage, and empower others to become firmly rooted in Jesus Christ for the advancement of God's Kingdom through the local Church and marketplace.

In his personal time, Mike enjoys biking, day trading, and huddling with family and friends.

Read more at https://radicalinchrist.com.

Milton Keynes UK
Ingram Content Group UK Ltd.
UKHW020936221123
433051UK00020B/1167

9 798223 300267